A Stranger at Your Door

Also by John Powell

Books:
    The John Powell Library
    Happiness is an Inside Job
    The Secret of Staying in Love
    Why Am I Afraid To Tell You Who I Am?
    Why Am I Afraid To Love?
    Will the Real Me Please Stand Up
    Fully Human, Fully Alive
    Through Seasons of the Heart
    Through the Eyes of Faith
    The Christian Vision
    Abortions: The Silent Holocaust
    He Touched Me
    A life-giving Vision

Audio Cassettes:
    Alcoholism
    Being a Fully Alive Person – Series I and II
    The Fully Alive Experience
    The Growing Edge of Life Series
    My Vision and My Values

Videos:
    Free to Be Me
    Happiness Is An Inside Job
    Why Am I Afraid To Tell You Who I Am?

John Powell

A Stranger at Your Door

ST PAULS

Unless otherwise stated all scripture quotations are taken from, or adapted from, the Good News Bible text, Today's English Version.
Copyright American Bible Society, 1993.

Cover Picture: William Holman Hunt's *The Light of the World* by permission of the Warden and Fellows of Keble College, Oxford.

ST PAULS
Morpeth Terrace, London SW1P 1EP

First published in 1997 by ST PAULS, UK-Eire

ISBN 085439 522 9

Produced in the EU
Printed by The Guernsey Press Company Ltd.

ST PAULS is an activity of the priests and brothers of the Society of St Paul who proclaim the Gospel through the media of social communication

Why you need this book...

Because of the:

- right reflections it forces you to make
- right results it can bring
- insights and ideas that will inspire and instruct you
- life giving questions it asks
- choices it will help you make
- key issues in it
- focus and force it has to help one live more fully
- combination of simplicity and solidness it contains

Acknowledgements

A book is a work of many hands and minds and hearts. Even in a work as small as this, there have been too many contributions of labour, encouragement, and generosity for specific mention of each.

A special word of gratitude to Clive H. Potter for his commendable efforts to render this work more relevant and rewarding for readers of the 21st Century.

John Powell, S.J.
Loyola University of Chicago
1998

Contents

Introduction

This book remains true to its original inspiration, namely:

◆ The presentation of the most important question in our life ... the decision about Christ, "the stranger at the door".

◆ To help people discern and decide what to do about "the stranger at the door".

◆ To encourage people to take time out to meditate on this important decision, what to do about "the stranger at the door".

To the reader

Since AD 30, all real thinking and intelligent living have forced upon people a fundamental decision. Since that time no thinker in the Christian world has considered the origin and destiny of life and been able to advance an intelligent theory, nor has any salesperson, mechanic, or executive settled upon a sound plan of life without somehow reckoning with the claims of Jesus of Galilee. The demands which this Jesus has always pressed upon the human mind and heart are not soft and malleable to the contours of human comfort. Like the man, Christ, they are not to be compromised. Partial acceptance of Christ is rejection of Christ. It is his own solemn determination:

> "He who is not with Me is against Me."

Every person whose life has been touched by Christianity and the claims of Christ, whatever their situation or station in life, has enjoyed the freedom of choice; but just as surely as one makes the journey over the road of life, one must sooner or later come to that fork which calls for acceptance or rejection of Christ. There is no middle path. Six billion human beings are now in the course of that journey. Each, if they are aware of Christ's claims, has a decision to make.

The importance of that decision is not minimised by the great number of people deciding. This is of paramount and eternal importance for every person; upon their decision will hinge everything. You and I, the person selling papers, the pilot, the bus driver, the elderly person who hobbles down the street, and the person next door practising music – we all must either take Christ in or we must rule him out. The book you are holding in your hands is a humble treatment of a magnificent theme: the divinity of Christ and the divine authority of His Church, proved especially from the miracles of the Gospels and Christianity. These are transcendent realities which demand profound consideration both by the person who has accepted to live by them and by the person who stands before these truths in humble inquiry and quest of certainty. The one who is living by these truths needs to be strengthened in his or her faith which will tend to grow weak unless bolstered up by such meditation as is here proposed. One who hesitates in the presence of these truths needs this reflection, too, in order to prepare himself or herself for the grace of faith and the acceptance of Christ's Church. A STRANGER AT YOUR DOOR is addressed to both these people, in the hope that it will help them to a happier and holier life, in and through Christ.

The pages that follow, you will find, cannot hope to impose a decision nor compel assent. Assent is exclusively yours to give or refuse. But if anyone shall find in these pages a stimulant to consider what will be the most important decision of his/her life, their purpose will have been achieved.

One important suggestion. Do not just read these pages. Study them, think about them, think around and beyond them. Turn whatever thoughts you find over and over in prayerful consideration. Let them mellow and ferment in the vats of your human mind and will. Such meditation will reward you richly. The latent energies of such a prayerful reading will reach long and wide and powerfully into your life. It will be the most important decision you have ever come to; a decision for eternity.

It is not a simple matter to struggle through the barbs and branches of thought that one might encounter in considering the claims and cause of Christ. It is so much easier to cuddle up to sleep in the depths of the forests of procrastination. But one does not find the clearing, the green slopes and flower-starred hills by shrinking from the enterprise of the trek. Nor will the sun ever break through the ceiling of such a world, and spill its warmth, joy, and light.

Chapter 1

The Timeless Question

Many years ago, the Jewish world could not make up its mind about a new prophet and wonder-worker. He was 'the carpenter's son', this Jesus of Galilee, and yet his words were more sublime and his deeds more mighty than any ever recorded in the annals of man. His was a challenge that could not be taken lightly. He asked a question, a very searching question, which pressed upon the hearts as well as the minds of people:

"Who do you say that I am?"

The question is timeless. It is directed at all peoples, with no reservations about time or place. It is directed at you and at me. We cannot ignore the question, any more than we can ignore the severe condition which Christ places on salvation: "No one," he said, "comes to the Father except through me."

"Who do you say that I am?"

An eternal destiny hangs in the balance as we decide how we are going to answer this all-important question.

In San Francisco, a regular customer sits in a bar, arguing in fuzzy tones and with threadbare platitudes.

In a shack of plain boards, at the foot of the Cumberlands, a little old lady sits with needle and thread.

In Washington DC there is a person who feels consumed by a multitude of knotty problems; he is waiting for a decision.

A pilot spans the wide Atlantic. His ears hear a melody amid the steady drone of four powerful engines.

In Paris, a young composer labours over a delicate *fugue*.

There is the bright hope of a pioneer in the heart of a youthful person in Australia.

A little schooner glides and bobs on Tokyo Bay and a young Argentinian adventurer feels free and daring.

> These people are very important to Christ, just as you and I are very important to him. However their preoccupations might seem to obscure this fact. Christ's grace is at work in their hearts. His grace is at work in your heart and in mine. He presses his question.

But there is a question, an old question.

It hangs on the crisp air, it penetrates the stale air of the bar room, lurks at the foot of the Cumberlands and whines over the motors of transport.

It repeats itself in the heart of Israel, steals through the door of the Parisian apartment, and floats over the waves of Tokyo Bay.

There is a stranger at the door.

He stands patiently; always at the door of the barracks; at the door of the Pentagon; outside the little Cumberland cottage.

He stands at every door which encloses the human soul.

He waits patiently for his opportunity. Days and weeks … months and years gather a meaningless dust.

Sooner or later, the soul will listen, and he will pose his question.

———◆◆◆◆◆———

There will be no variation. He will put the question as simply and as forcefully as he once did, so long ago, in Caesarea Philippi.

Who do you say that I am?

> All really great people have wrestled with the problem of human destiny. Only sound convictions about one's own destiny produce hearts that are able to love life dearly and yet still be glad to die. No one today will possess these sound convictions until they have answered the question of Christ.

We can ignore this question.

But ignoring it can be more destructive than the havoc of a flood; more catastrophic than the atomic fission that was set off over Hiroshima.

And yet there are many answers. Error is possible.

But the heart that utters error in answer may be sealed into eternal doom and gloom.

Such error kills and blinds. It creates a thousand thorns of torture. It leaves the human soul in a horrible void, without nourishment. And where there is no nourishment, atrophy and decay will set in.

It is a foolish thing to look up quickly at this stranger. A snap judgement can be a lethal judgement. Error is too costly.

We can override our mistakes, almost always, if we have the heart to begin again. A public figure can regain the public's confidence even though this may have been lost due to poor judgement. An actress may have delivered a lifeless sequence of lines and lost her audience but she can always regain their attention with an improved performance.

And yet when human judgement has rejected the stranger who stands at the door of the human heart, there is no other way. The road to their destiny is blocked off. That person then travels at his or her own great risk.

Human destiny is a weighty mystery.

No matter what we personally think about human destiny, we must learn to accept its fundamental importance and acknowledge the pivotal role of "historical facts".

We honour Socrates, Plato and Aristotle. We honour all those minds of profound insight which have sought, over the years, to unravel this mystery.

These men have written their beliefs in stone and on papyrus. They have left their hopes on canvas and reams of paper. But never more eloquently than in human blood; blood that coursed from hearts that were in love with an ideal.

Reminiscences:

There was Socrates calmly swallowing the hemlock; thousands of brave souls pouring out their lives in the gory Roman arenas; Ignatius of Antioch longing to become the food of the lions; and the little 'Maid of Orleans' who was burned at the stake.

People do not become martyrs for whims and for fancies.

Heroes are not born on the fluff of featherbeds. They are born on crosses, in fires, by swords.

Nor is there a solitary soul that has ever sounded with the ring of greatness that was without a deep belief, a deep belief in human destiny, right or wrong.

———◆◈◆———

The stranger is still at the door.

His lips forever form the timeless question.

But the heart of the hearer sighs. The boy goes back to his toy guns; the drinker returns to his drink; the diplomat focuses his mind yet again upon his decisions; the pilot checks his readings, and the little old lady is still absorbed in her stitches.

Human destiny hangs precariously on the unanswered question of the stranger at the door.

These human destinies are deferred for the moment.

He has hardly been noticed.

The origin of the question. Jesus puts the question to his apostles. Peter's answer.

Once, sitting around a fire – a solitary ball of light – in the darkness of Caesarea Philippi in Galilee, the stranger at the door sat with a group of disciples. Genesareth lapped softly in the distance.

They were a group of motley souls. Their bodies reeked with the odour of fish, and the flames of the fire played distortions upon their weather-beaten and intense faces.

Then it was, two thousand years into the past – before the age of transport; before the advent of telecommunications, videos and television screens – that the question was born!

"Now Jesus, having come into the district of

Caesarea Philippi, began to ask his disciples the question, saying: 'Who do men say the Son of Man is?'"

The faces of the men, huddled around the warmth of the fire, were masked with doubt. They looked from one to another, waiting for the first person to offer an answer.

Finally, one of the bronzed faces leaned forward: "Some say John the Baptist; and others, Elijah; and others, Jeremiah or one of the prophets."

There was a pause.

Even these simple fishermen knew what was to follow, and each prepared his answer.

One studied his rough hands, calloused heavily from mending fishing nets. Another found sudden concern in the crackle and glow of the fire.

"But who do you say that I am?" came the inevitable question.

The fisherman who had been studying his hands raised his head slowly. His answer was deliberate. How many times he had turned the question over in his mind.

He said simply: "You are the Christ, the Son of the living God."

There was nothing to be added, no qualification. There had been no note of conjecture in his voice.

Those rough hands had truth in their firm grasp.

The waters of the distant Genesareth lapped quietly against the sandy shores.

So many chains of reasoning about human destiny have been forged upon the anvil of the human heart with the tireless blows of the human mind. So many of our best minds have looked sadly upon their reasonings, finding them incomplete. These were razor-sharp minds and theirs were herculean efforts; but for all their facility with the scales and balances of logic, there was no cornerstone; there was no Christ.

O simple fisherman, how could you know?

How could you know that the link of truth which great minds have grasped for was solidly locked in your callous-crusted hands?

"You are the Christ, the Son of the living God!"

Down through the arch of the centuries Christ continues to press people for an answer to his question. But not all people have the insight of Peter, and the rejection that culminated in Calvary is repeated on a daily basis because people will not consider Christ's claims.

The drama did not end with the last flicker of that fire which lit up the faces of Christ and his apostles.

The curtain has not fallen yet.

It has not fallen in Caesarea Philippi. It has

not fallen in Bosnia, nor in Washington, Paris, or Israel.

As long as new human life is given and formed in the wombs of women, as long as there are human hearts and human souls, the curtain shall not fall.

The acts and scenes are in endless change.

But the climax is not yet.

There is still a 'little one'.

And "it is not the will of your Father in heaven that a single one of these little ones should perish" ... in Bosnia, in San Francisco, in Washington, Paris, or in Moscow.

It is obvious that the world will always have a stranger at its door.

And a timeless, ageless question, forever waiting to be answered:

"Who do you say that I am?"

———◆◆◆◆———

When Peter confessed so simply, so directly (and so beautifully) that Christ was the Son of God, the heart of Christ was warm with happiness.

But the saddest line had yet to be written.

It would be so different from the note of recognition in Caesarea Philippi.

He would come and he would go, and one who loved him with a strong love would write the story of his failure: "He came unto his own, and his own received him not."

He has come to so many millions of people, only to be rejected.

He has come holding in his hands the power for people to become the sons of God. ("… but to those who received him, he gave them the power to become the sons of God.")

The tragedy here is unmistakable. It is worse than sightless eyes; worse than stories of human agony and grief which are buried under the wrecks of fire and flood. It is more hideous than the stretchers which follow in the wake of war, and the smashed humanity which they support.

> "In him was life …
> And the life was the light of the world …
> And the light shineth in the darkness of the world …
> And the darkness did not comprehend it."
> "He was in the world,
> And the world was made by him,
> And the world knew him not."

Dear soldier in Bosnia, look up from the guns which you have levelled at your enemy;

People at the bar, give your mind and heart a chance;

Dear woman, look up from your computer;

Mr Diplomat, there is a far more important decision to be made by you;

Look up, Paris, Israel, Russia, Tokyo;

Listen again, pilot ... to the voices inside;
There is a stranger at your door;
There is the all-important question to be answered;
Human destiny rides tremulously upon that answer of yours;
Eternal destiny.

This is a destiny beyond the dirt and rains of shores;
Beyond the bar of hard oak; far more warming than your shot of rye.
This is a destiny to be lived, after the Cumberlands have been worn away;
A goal beyond paltry diplomatic conundrums;
A vision to outlast Israel and China.
It is more beautiful than the sun flashing on your silver wings;
Deeper and wider, more vast and lovely than the waters of the Mediterranean, or the great, restless Pacific.

Dear reader of these lines, look up!
There is a stranger at your door.
In him is life;
The life that can be the light of your world.
He is the Way, the Truth, and the Life.
There is a question to be answered. Look up.

Chapter 2

The Stranger's Claim

For us to answer the timeless question intelligently, an intuition of the heart is not enough. Before we place our trust in anyone, we wisely demand certain credentials, and we ask for definite information. Consequently, the question is logical here: What were Christ's credentials? What was his mission? Was the human race, in any sense, expecting Christ's coming? For the answer to these questions, we must go back to the creation of the world, and to the great sin of Adam. Adam had been the delight of God at the moment of his creation. He was not destined to live forever in the garden of Eden. In fact, he was to undergo a temporary probation which would finally admit him to the most blessed vision of God; to the eternal bliss of Heaven. By his sin of disobedience, however, God's plan was marred. Adam had wilfully cast away the friendship of his maker, and the gates of Heaven were then closed to Adam and his children. But the mercy of God comes to people in the hope-filled message of the prophets. Christ's coming, and his atonement for the sin of Adam and for the sins of people, is the great Good News, or gospel of the Old Testament.

Anyone who seeks admission to someone's home must have credentials. The same is true, but in a more important way, of the people who seek admission to our hearts – the people who demand our love.

A woman is busy with her cleaning. All the dust and dirt brought into her house by three mischievous children must be fought to an unconditional surrender.

But all the dust and dirt she fights is not safely gathered into the dustpan. Smudges of it are on her face. The bandanna, with which she has tied up her hair, bears marks of the battle, too.

There is only one thing to say: she is a mess.

Now, as we all know very well, when we look a mess, someone always comes to call.

This occasion is no exception. Someone rings the front door bell.

This is a signal for quick action: the bandanna flutters to the floor … the apron is placed behind the kitchen door on a well-concealed hook … anxious hands fluff out the hair, and then run quickly over the face (making those smudges into streaks).

It is now or never, and so she goes to the door with an unbelievable air of calm; no one would ever guess that she had been agitated, ruffled … especially the man who is standing at the door … a man she has never seen before.

How could anyone be expected to see

through this air of poise and pretended calm, as she says:

"Good afternoon."

But she is not thinking, "Good afternoon."

She is thinking, "Who are you? Why are you here? ... especially now when I'm so busy."

"Oh yes, of course. We've been expecting you. Your company said they'd arrange for someone to call. The television hasn't been working for days. It's just in here."

Without hesitation or doubt she leads him through her topsy-turvy sanctuary.

He was expected; he came as promised; he identified himself properly.

All is well.

Soon the television will be working again.

All is routine. But if the man at the door had not been expected, if he had not been able to identify himself, he could not have taken a step into that house.

The stranger at the door ... Is he expected? Can he identify himself? Why has he come? Why is he waiting there?

"I have come so that you might have life – life in all its fullness."

To understand the coming and the mission of Christ we have to turn back the pages of history until we are alone in that solemn silence when only God existed.

Digression is the only choice.

The book of human history is a large, heavy book.

This book is so large and so heavy that it has never found a life long enough, or an author daring enough, to carry out its research and its writing.

Historians are excused from knowing the whole book. Any one chapter that has been mastered wins the diploma of approval.

With a sigh of unreal regret, we take this great, imaginary book into our hands. We place it on the floor and from a standing position begin to turn the pages.

We start from the back ... where the ink is not yet dry, and the sentence not yet finished. These last pages are more familiar anyway.

The last pages are of paper, but others are of cloth, pressed leaves and reeds, bronze, and finally, tablets of stone.

We begin the backward journey to seek the beginnings of human history.

The pages are lifted with effort and care.

As we proceed with the arduous task, the names, places, and events grow less and less familiar. Soon we are walking upon unfamiliar soil. The milestones become more and more confusing.

There is doubt at this point: Will we be able to finish it?

Then, just before the end – really it's the beginning – there's a reward.

A familiar name: Adam.

Adam, the father of all people; the father of work and pain, suffering and death. The father of thirst and hunger; the father of a thousand miseries; the father of hospitals; of every cry that has ever pierced the night; the father of insanity; the father of cemeteries and courts of law; the father of all the evil riot in our bodies; the father of the darkness and of the chaos in our souls.

But, for all that, our father.

We must not hate. We cannot disown.

———◆◆◆◆◆———

With a silent satisfaction the front cover is turned.

The book is closed once again.

We now stand alone. We stand, before the first word of history could be written … before the world we have known … before the mountains and the valleys … before the first gigantic wave of the ocean rammed against a shoal … before the first bird gave music to the world … before the first howl of passion was heard from within the depths of the jungle … before the first footprint of a person … before Orion and the Milky Way … before the endless, depthless blue and before the blazing sun.

We are alone.

But we are not alone.

"… before the world was made, I am!"

In the whirl and toss and roll of imagination we can wipe away all else. But he is! God is.

The infinite, eternal, almighty God.

What was it like?

Was he lonely without the world at his feet? A foolish thing to think about an infinite God; infinite in his joy, his ecstasy of love; happy beyond the most daring sweep of imagination.

We have passed the limit, the foremost limit, of the book.

We cannot go beyond the author.

We can never go beyond the pen that did the writing, the prime originality from which all things have come: the infinite love of him, who before the length and breadth and depth of all creation is …

> We stand with God at the sacred moment when he brought into being all things that have being: the creation of the world.

This was the love, the power, the wisdom that, in the beginning, spilled and overflowed.

> "In the beginning God created heaven and earth.
> And the earth was void and empty, and darkness was upon the face of the deep.
> And the spirit of God moved over the waters.
> And God said: 'Be there light!'
> And light was made.
> And God saw the light that it was good; and he

divided the light from the darkness.
And he called the light, day, and the darkness, night.
And there was evening and morning one day.
And God said: Let there be a firmament made
amidst the waters and let it divide the waters
from the waters.
And God called the dry land earth; and the gathering
together of the waters he called seas.
And God saw that it was good.
And he said: Let us make man and woman to our
image and likeness; and let them have dominion
over the fishes of the sea, and the fowls of the air,
and the beasts, and the whole earth.
And God saw all the things that he had made, and
they were very good."

All in the flash and thunder of an almighty will!

Be there waters! Blue and pure waters. Large, rolling bodies of restlessness. The ripple and skip of streams. The placid lakes over which the trinket of his moon may lay a strip of yellow ribbon, when day is done and the sun has set.

Be there earth! Deep, rich soil. Long rolls of fertility. Majestic snow-capped mountains to stand like kings over his plains and meadows. Carpets of restful green. Clusters of flower and vine. (Be enchanting, earth. Be a legacy and a message: tell the life placed in your support how beautiful is he, who "before the world was created ... is.")

Be there a human being! The crown of creation. The image and likeness of their author. Made to love and be loved. Sharer in the life of God himself. Led by an irresistible instinct. Formed by Love to return love.

———◆◆◆◆◆———

It is good to go back, to stand thoughtfully at the place of our origin.

It is good to go back and kneel silently at the feet of our God.

> The story of creation and man and woman, the lord of creation, is marked by an almost immediate catastrophe: the terrible sin of our first parents, Adam and Eve.

Our hands are back at the heavy pages of history. We have looked with eyes full of amazement upon the almost unbelievable act which we call creation.

Where before there was nothing, absolute nothing, there is now a vast and wonderful universe — flowers, hillsides, brute beasts, and ... two human beings.

Our hands are back at the pages of history, back through the story's beginning, back through the story of Adam and Eve.

Back over that terrible line: "... you have eaten of the tree whereof I commanded you that you should not eat!"

Here, for the first time, the sword of sin is thrust into the side of God.

But it was human blood that flowed from the wound in answer.

Every child that is brought forth upon God's earth shall bear the scar of that wound, and wear the badge of his parent's rebellion.

But there is a deeper grief.

The doors of this world swing wide.

But the doors of heaven are sealed and it is beyond our power to open them.

The doors of home are closed. Heaven is barred; we have lost our home.

The beauty that once charmed the very eye of God – the beauty of his own reflection – is an orphaned beauty; made parentless and homeless by our own cleavage. It is beyond human repair.

This is the deeper grief: we cannot go home. (Think of it. Think of this sorrow: to be barred from home!)

The familiar sounds are never to be heard again. The longed for sights will not be seen. The voice, desired by the deepest roots of instinct, will be forever silent.

There is no warmth, no solace – alienated from parents and from home.

The night is cold.

And our lonely hearts cannot plead for justice. Justice has been done: it is beyond us to do anything about it.

Our hands still turn pages …

The prophets of the Old Testament were men whom God inspired to interpret the mind and will of God for their people. Through the voice of the prophets God gave the world renewed hope. He gave us a great expectancy that mercy and forgiveness would be brought to the world. God would send the Messiah.

Hearts without hope wander blindly down the dark streets of human history.

Then ... a light flickers briefly in the distance.

Hope is reborn. Hope courses through the once-frozen veins of the corpse of the human race. One, who is born of woman, shall open the door which shall lead us from our exile.

One, who is born of woman, shall open the door to home. "I will put enmities between thee and the woman, and thy seed and her seed; she shall crush thy head."

This God says to the serpent of doom.

And the voice of our great God resounds against the breast of the patriarch, Abraham: "I will make thee a great nation ... and in thee shall all nations (all the kindred of the earth) be blessed."

... The kindred of the earth shall be blessed. Blessed with the mercy of a father, our Father.

But how? How can mercy surmount the high wall of eternal justice?

Jacob lays new and live coals on the fire of hope: "Juda, thee shall thy brethren praise.... The sceptre shall not be taken away from Juda, nor a ruler from his thigh, till he comes that is to be sent, and he shall be the expectation of nations."

God will not leave us as orphans.

"A star shall rise out of Jacob and a sceptre shall spring up from Israel!"

The voice of the psalmist raises the prophetic message to a new pitch of hope: "Thou art my son, this day have I begotten thee.... I will give thee the nations for thy inheritance."

"He shall protect the lowly among the people, he shall save the children of the poor, and shall crush the oppressor."

God will send mercy to his people.

Not riding on the condescension of written decree;

Not through the sound of human voices.

God shall himself inhabit our land of darkness and tears.

As a child he shall come.

"A child is born to us, and a son is given to us, and the government is upon his shoulders; and his name shall be called Wonderful-Counsellor, God the Mighty, the Father of the world to come, the Prince of Peace!"

He will come clothed in our human inheritance. He will feel the weight of our woes.

He will conquer by blood ... his own blood:

"I was as a meek lamb, that is carried to be a victim."

Here is the resurrection of hope.

Here is hope at its brightest.

Here in the prophetic visions, uttered by tongues that have felt the purifying sting of live coals.

The voice of the prophet splits the midnight sky of despair. Hope sends a wedge of light screaming earthward ... into the heavy hearts of people.

God shall send the Son that he has begotten!

The gaping birthmark of Adam's sons will be cleansed from the foreheads of people. The wound shall be closed.

The gulf, the infinite gulf, that has separated us from our true home shall be spanned by a new bridge of mercy.

Even if tears of gratitude coursed down the furrowed cheeks of the human race, it would be understandable.

There is warmth and joy in the very thought: once more we are able to go home!

The hope-bearing voice of the prophet: Look to your horizons, Juda. One day, with the setting of the sun, a star shall arise out of thy bosom, O Jacob.

He will come "that is to be sent"!

"Protector of the lowly ... the expectation of the nations ... the inheritance of the nations ... the Son whom God has begotten ... Salvation of the children of the poor ... Crusher of the oppressor ...

Wonderful-Counsellor, God the Mighty ... Father of the world to come ... Prince of Peace!"

"A child shall be born to thee!"

Born in the helpless form of a child.

Born to die. Born for victimhood. Born to be the lamb led to slaughter.

Rejoice, fallen heart of a person, for in the death of that lamb you may find life!

> The prophecies find their fulfilment in the most solemn moment this world has ever known: the Incarnation of the Eternal Word of God. The Son of God becomes a man.

This was the prophecy. This was the refurbished hope, the confirmation that there would be a stranger at the doors of the world. It would be a thousand years before he would appear; a thousand years of hope; a thousand years of counting, marking time; like counting beads, knowing that you will reach the end and that the gem will be fastened there.

A thousand years of hope – a thousand pages later in the history of the human race – our hands fly through the pages ... the words of confirmation. The prophecies are fulfilled. (Long into the past, a thousand miles back on the highways of history, like a sound of rising from the loneliest grave, the quivering voice of the hoary prophet had said: "Behold the Virgin shall be with Child. And she shall bring forth a Son!")

The confirmation so long in coming strikes like thunder at the heart which pounds wildly in the breast of humankind.

Ah! There it is. There it is beyond denying: The angel has spoken to a little maiden in Galilee. "Behold you will conceive in your womb, and shall bring forth a Son, and you shall call his name … Jesus!"

———◆◆◆———

This was the moment; an angel and a maiden; and a human race and human hope hanging on the words of the maiden.

Quietly she spells out the hope of man: "Behold the handmaid of the Lord. Be it done unto me according to thy word!"

———◆◆◆———

And in that instant: "The Word was made flesh."

A colloquy addressed to Mary, the Immaculate Mother of God, whose thoughts are searched as she holds her newly-born child close to her heart, in the manger at Bethlehem.

All this, even this, thousands of years after the first painful surge of hope and expectation had awakened the hearts of Adam's children. "…She brought forth her first-born son, and wrapped him in swaddling clothes, and laid him in a manger …"

———◆◆◆———

Young Mother, as you looked upon those tiny hands, did you see them extended to all ages to come? Did you see them at work with hammer and nails in the carpenter's shop? Did you see them raised, beautiful with power and majesty, to still the squall over Genesareth? Did you see them holding the bread that was to become his body, the cup and covenant of his blood? Did you see those tiny hands brimming, running over with forgiveness for his 'little ones'? Did you see those tiny hands and feet covered with blood on Mount Calvary? Did you see them reaching out to the last person that will ever live on this earth?

As you wrapped those tiny feet … Did you know how tirelessly they would pursue the hearts of people over the dusty roads of Galilee and the world? Did you know they would walk the pavements of Houston, Chicago, and Paris; the cobbled roads of Amsterdam, Rome, and ancient Bruges? Did you know that they would board all the ships in the harbours? Did you see them tramping the boulevards and back streets of the world, pressing through jungle paths, along every human-made way? Did you see them standing at every mansion and gas-lit tenement? Did you see them at the doorstep? Their hands were filled with mercy. Their feet were made to follow. Wherever there is a 'little one' there he will be – this, thy son, young mother, a stranger at every door, behind which there is a human soul and a human heart, and human sickness and human grief. Did you know that this was the reason he had come?

> The stranger at your door comes uniquely announced through the voices of the prophets. No other figure in history has come heralded in this way; nor is it possible, except by the intervention of God, who thus sends his eternal Son into the world that we might recognise him and claim him as our Messiah and Saviour.

Dear women, busy with your Saturday cleaning, the stranger standing at your door has come uniquely announced. He has been expected with an expectation as old as the Garden of Eden.

The Expectation of the Nations, he has come to you, to claim the rightful debt of your heart.

We may search our minds ... we may search the long and large book of human history, but we shall find none other that comes as he has come. Ask the names and the places that we remember from school:

> Julius Caesar, who were your prophets?
> Gustavus Adolphus, how could we have expected you?
> Where was the notice of your coming, Bonaparte?
> Were you the expectation of your people, Disraeli?
> Bismarck, did you carry any credentials other than your insatiable lust for 'steel and blood'?
> Were the people of France ever told to look to you, little island of Corsica?

What was the truth about you, Arpinum? Did you
know that Cicero would immortalise your name?

If you think too long about these questions,
they will disturb you.

The realisation will startle you. You will have
to face it even if you don't like or want it.

The truth of it will not be obscured. Sometimes the eyes can hide their tears, but the mind
of man is fashioned for greater honesty.

Here was a life 'written' before it was lived!

Here was a man whose biographers might
have been his most ancient forebears. Here was a
narration before the narrative.

You could say 'fantastic anachronism' but it is
really too fantastic.

We are here face to face with the Almighty, in
whose hand alone the answer lies. The mouth of
the prophet opened, but the voice was the voice
of God.

David, Isaiah, Jeremiah, Daniel,
Micah, Zacharias, Malachi:
How else could you know?
How else could your dim eyes have focused on the
little town of Bethlehem in Judea?
How else could you have listed an as yet unbegotten
genealogy – an unlived descent?
How could you know:
Born of a virgin?
Announced by the 'voice of one crying in the
wilderness'?
How could you see him entering Jerusalem? How

could you know the power in his hands? How could the silhouette of a cross not yet erected cast its shadow back over the centuries to be seen by your eyes?

Yet these are the facts.

This is the gist: a life was written, by the prophetic inspiration of God, even before that life was lived!

Working mother, mechanic, salesperson, student: take down the family heirloom (the Bible) which stands in the bookcase. Take down David, Isaiah, Jeremiah; take down Daniel, Micah, and Zacharias. Read thoughtfully for yourself. These are very old words that you will read, grey with the greyness of three thousand years. But their meaning is as fresh as the current moment.

Read and think, and …

Go to the door! Go to the expectation of the nations, the meek lamb of God, the star risen out of little Nazareth.

Yes, the expectation of all the nations of the world really and truly is waiting at your door … a stranger at your door.

This is the One of whom God said, through the prophet Isaiah:

"Behold my servant. I will uphold him.
My elect: my soul delights in him.
I have given my spirit upon him.
He shall bring forth judgement to the Gentiles
… He shall be no respecter of persons.

He shall bring forth judgement unto truth.
… And the islands shall wait for his law.
… I have given thee for a covenant of the people,
For a light of the Gentiles.
That thou mightiest open the eyes of the blind,
And bring forth the prisoner out of the prison,
And them that sit in darkness out of the dungeon."

It is important to you that the 'elect of God' should stand at your doorstep. It means so much more than your set of ceramics, in which you take such well-deserved pride; more than your guns, polished and ready for the season to open; more than your drinks and discussions; more than your bridge sessions and your season pass to the opera.

It is far more necessary for you to know this and do something about it than for you to take twenty per cent from that last sale, which you negotiated so cleverly, or for you to enjoy that weekend in Florida, which has sparked your imagination.

The instincts which have forever driven great thinkers to seek an answer and solution to the great problems of human life, and which drive every one of us who wants to find some meaning in our day-to-day lives, can be satisfied only by One: the Alpha and Omega; the beginning and the end; the Messiah, the Christ.

Thoughtful people have dipped deep beneath the shiny surface waters of life to find that truth which alone can satisfy the hungry human heart, and so many have sadly come up with sand in their thirsty mouths: with Brahma, Krishna, Varuna, Buddha; with Zeus, Mazda, and the sun-god.

Do not laugh at them. While others were making gods of sex and stomach, and (in spite of what Copernicus would discover) making themselves the centre of the universe, these people were in search of something; in search of a cornerstone which had not been laid.

Our generation uncovers the same instincts in people, but in a different way.

Our generation parades ceremoniously, and unabashed, to go and lie on the psychiatrist's couch.

But the urge and instinct in them and in us is one and the same.

We are looking for a meaning, for a reality: we do not know what it is or where we may find it, but that thirst and pain drive us to the four corners of the earth to find something that has, in fact, been waiting at the door.

This decision at our doorstep; this concern at our threshold; this Messiah ... this Christ.

The thrill of discovery awaits the opening of the door; the thrill of recognition. The thrill of a man named Andrew, who once raced breathlessly over a road in Bethany beyond the Jordan, to tell his brother the news – the news which is at your door – "We have found the Messiah!"

The meaning for Andrew and Peter, the

meaning for you and me, is one and the same!

The same hope.
The same salvation.
The Hebrew tongue called him their 'Messiah'.
The Greek-speaking people called him their 'Christ'.

There is one great thing in your life:
He belongs to no one more than to you!

The story that follows is the story related in the Gospel of St John about the meeting of Jesus and the Samaritan woman at the well of Jacob. Although she is slow to understand, the patient Jesus at last succeeds in telling her that he is the expected Messiah.

One bright and hot day, Jesus was passing through a little town, called Sichar, in the district of Samaria in Palestine. The journey on foot from Judea had been long and tiring, and the remainder of the journey to Galilee was not a happy prospect for the blistered and burning feet of the little group that travelled with the Master.

So they found their way to an ancient landmark in Sichar, called very simply, 'The Well of Jacob'. It was a deep, refreshing shaft of water for which the villagers gave thanks to their father, Jacob. The hallowed tradition, which became known far and wide, was that the grand old patriarch had bequeathed this well to his son, Joseph, and to all the thirsty flock of natives that would come there to draw water for the following day.

It had become a 'town square' long before the days of town squares, where many a bronze-skinned peasant first made the acquaintance of his neighbour. These simple folks had no super-markets, office buildings, or social clubs. These familiar institutions would be the social arsenal of a different and distant age.

Here it was, then, by the side of this sunken cylinder of grey stone, that he sat for a moment of rest.

The virtuous disciples had hurried off to the town proper to buy some food.

Jesus was alone in the hot sun, awaiting the visitor who had been appointed by divine provi-dence from all eternity.

Jauntily, over the parched road, carrying a water jar on her head, she came. A Samaritan woman, she was a stranger to him, just as he would be to her.

She was a complete extrovert, this woman; born out of her time.

Had she dwelt among our skyscraping giants of steel and stone, she would have raised many an eyebrow in the circles of polite society.

As she approached, she stole a quick glance at the stranger who was sitting by the side of the well.

Her ever urgent impulse to conversation vapourised in that glance.

No one could mistake him. He was a Jew!

And even Jews who are lost would not stoop

to ask a Samaritan for directions, let alone exchange a pleasant 'hello'.

And she, being a Samaritan and proud of it, bore a disdain similar to the disdain she had projected into his mind.

So she grasped the rope at Jacob's well with routine facility, and while she was fastening the end of the rope to her pail, a soft surprise came from the side of the well: "Would you please give me a drink?"

Her eyes widened in surprise, and she fixed them suddenly on this man. Perhaps she had been a bit hasty in her judgement. Perhaps this man was not really a Jew.

The second survey confirmed the first.

She cleared her throat and said: "How is it that you, although you are a Jew, ask me for a drink ... me, a Samaritan woman?"

For all the pointedness in her question, she was hardly ready for this: "If you only knew the gift of God, and who it is that is saying to you 'Give me a drink,' you perhaps would have asked of him, and he would have given you living water." (Could he expect her to know that 'in him was life'? Could she be made to wonder?) Her answer immediately deflated all hopes for any wonder or understanding:

"Sir, this well is deep, and you have nothing to draw with. So where could you get this living water?"

Her mind was sadly fastened to the thought of the water that can be ladled into a jar. "Are you greater than our father Jacob who gave us the well, and drunk from it himself, and his sons, and his flocks?"

His answer was directly to the point: "Everyone who drinks of this water will thirst again. He, however, who drinks of the water that I will give shall never thirst; but the water that I will give him will become in him a fountain of water, springing up unto life everlasting."

He is holding out to her the life of the spirit, a life of devotion and worship. He is holding out to her the quite indescribable gift which we call a participation in the life of God. It is the only water that will quench the thirst of a human soul.

But her mind does not see what it is that he offers. She still thinks in terms of water as in Jacob's well. She foolishly imagines that he is going to give her a supply of that water which will save her the hot wearisome trip to 'Jacob's Well'.

"Sir, give me this water that I may not thirst, or come here to draw."

You or I would have given her up as hopeless.

You or I would have impatiently regretted bringing the subject up, and we might have dismissed the subject with a casual, "It's been hot today, hasn't it?"

But you and I do not wait at doors that will never open, either.

He sees one alternative.

He will make her see the power that could cause a hundred wells to come gushing from the arid deserts of Samaria.

"Go call your husband, and come here."

"I have no husband."

"You have said well, 'I have no husband' for you have had five husbands, and he whom you have now is not your husband. In this you have spoken truly."

Then, there was dawn in that mind, bright and clear.

"Sir, I see you are a prophet. Our fathers worshipped on this mountain, but you say that at Jerusalem is the place where one ought to worship."

He explains softly and simply that salvation will come to the world from among the Jews.

(Never would this woman stand so close to her salvation. Somewhere her soul is still living. It must be that if she is among the blessed in heaven, her salvation grew out of this day, this hour, these words that he spoke to her.)

"God is spirit, and they who worship him must worship in spirit and truth."

He struggles to make her see that living is not completely external. Neither is worship completely external. Such people, as this simple Samaritan woman, can talk in terms of water, because it slakes the thirst; water weighs, cools, washes, and extinguishes fire. The senses can argue to this. But there is more to worshipping and loving God than the argument of the senses. There is the heart which only God sees. We must kneel. We must offer prayers. We must worship gathered together, in a body (God promised to bless that prayer where two or three are gathered together in his name); – but all these things must be a reflection of that which God alone can see: the heart.

But she is sadly poor at subtleties: "I know that the Messiah is coming (who is called Christ), and when he comes he will tell us all things."

She has demolished any hope of indirectness or suggestion.

And so he says it simply and directly:

In a sense which is very real we are all typified by the Samaritan woman who met Jesus at Jacob's well. Like her we are all seekers. Like her, we may pray, we shall find Jesus and all search shall be ended for us.

St John tells us that the poor woman went off in such a hurry to tell the others in the little village that she left her water jar behind her.

We might wonder why St John bothered to record this fact. We might wonder if there isn't in this small thing a grand significance.

Each of us has a water jar ... an empty water jar.

We wander through life, wanting to find and to fill our jar.

The water that this man seeks is money. His neighbour seeks the cooling draughts of fame and honour. His brother has eyes only for the flow of hilarity that round after round of sex, liquor, and song deceitfully promise.

And each is met by a stranger at the well of his or her desires.

And each is promised: Who drinks of the water that I will give shall never thirst! The water that I shall give shall become in you a fountain of water, springing up into life everlasting.

But law shackles life ... and so, in the driving pains of our thirst, we sometimes make gods of sex, of our money, or of one or other well-coddled passion. We sometimes make one of these our Messiah.

And the springs at which we drink poison 'our souls.

But there is just enough Samaritan thickness in us to miss the point completely ... to forget (as we all forget at times):

"The water that I will give shall become in you a fountain of water, springing up into life everlasting."

We forget the stranger who waits so patiently at our door.

Some day, we must pray, the bright and clear

dawn will break, and we will happily leave our water jars at the wells of this world, and race breathlessly to announce to all that will hear: I have found the Messiah ... I have found the Christ!

This is what makes the acceptance or rejection of Jesus a thing of awesome importance to a person: they may be dealing with God. In fact, only God would press the demands upon a person that Jesus did not hesitate to impose. Still, the honest and teachable person has every right to ask Christ to prove his claims. It is, in fact, the part of intelligent faith, which is the faith that God honours in the Christian believer.

But these are the days of overstated advertisements.

Our grandmothers talked about a 'grain of salt'.

We are the 'salt-barrel' generation, then.

If housewives bought all the gadgets which 'will literally cut your housework in half', there would soon be no drudgery for the queen of the castle.

If our new cars were the ones advertised, re-pair shops would soon be closed for want of repairs.

This 'salt-barrel' generation is well schooled.

The simple fact with us is: Prove it!

Wrongly or rightly, we feel that the knocks and bumps of twenty centuries have made of us a progeny of sceptics, but in fact three-dimension is not new. We are not the first to say: 'I have to see it with my own eyes'.

The eyes of ancient Jerusalem wore three-dimensional glasses, and the minds we sometimes slough off as 'outmoded' thought of length and breadth and depth, long before our modern physicist found them one day in his laboratory.

Such were the eyes … such were the minds that first reckoned with the acceptance or rejection of Jesus of Galilee.

He could profess to the woman of Samaria that he was her Messiah … he could pronounce that Apostle (Peter) blessed who proclaimed him to be "… the Christ, the Son of the living God."

When the Jews demanded to know whether or not he was the Messiah, the Christ, he could answer them with: "I tell you and you do not believe!"

He could console the grief-stricken sister of the dead Lazarus with his claim: "I am the resurrection and the life; he who believes in me, even if he die, shall live; and whoever lives and believes in me, shall never die!" (… words which only God can rightly say!)

In the face of an agonising death, he could tell the Jewish Sanhedrin, in whose hands his fate rested, that he was the Christ, the Son of God; and he could boldly add that someday each of them would stand before his judgement.

He could lift up the sagging hearts of his disciples on the road to Emmaus with his explanation of how 'the Christ' (himself) had to suffer these things before entering into his glory....

But, before we can be expected to leave our precious water jars, to go in search of 'living waters'... he must prove it!

We do not say this with the cunning of a professional sceptic.

There is no cynicism, disguised or outright, in this demand.

No more than the child, whose wide eyes are gradually opening to the world of persons and things ... whose innocence we may have lost, but whose honest curiosity we share.

We want to be saved from the dishonest pretence, and stripped of that sophistication which humans sometimes wear like a new dress or a suit of clothes. We want to be washed of all malice.

But, we still ask: Why? Why must I accept the Christ?

This is indeed no simple matter. This is not a matter of days or weeks; or months or years.

This is not as ephemeral as last Saturday night's canasta game, the score of which escapes us at the moment (it was close, anyway).

The demands of Christ – the demands which Christ writes into the contract with his believer –

are not as forgettable as the phone bill last Christmas.

This is a question of eternity ... a measureless, endless existence, where the stakes are high, success unbelievable and failure irreparable and eternal!

This is a question of an eternal joy that 'eye hath not seen nor ear heard ...'

This is a question of everlasting fire.

Christ's demands are not for Sunday or Monday, for this week or that ... there is no time clause in the contract.

Christ comes saying that he teaches and confers life ... he speaks of the Kingdom of Heaven as his very own ... the Kingdom of God is his right ... he insists without compromise that whoever shall believe his teaching (and in him) shall be saved ... who will not believe will be damned into everlasting, unquenchable fire ... he says that his every word is the word of God because he is the Son of God ... he is God: "I and the Father are one!"

Oh no, my soul, this is not a simple matter.

Let us review the claims that Christ made to people. It would be a foolish thing to make any judgement of Christ without first considering carefully what he said about himself. We cannot say that Christ was merely a very holy man if he said he was God. There is no middle ground here. Either Christ was what he claimed to be and therefore worthy of all our love or he was an impostor and worthy only of the pity and compassion we give to deceivers.

Christ claimed to be the Messiah.

"I who speak with you am he," he told the Samaritan woman. Now, to the Messiah, in Hebrew tradition, belonged the honour and worship of all people. The very name, Christ, is the Greek equivalent of the Hebrew, Messiah. Consequently, each time that he used this name (Christ) or accepted its usage, he affirmed that he was the Messiah.

Christ claimed to be a teacher, sent from God to teach a divine religion.

"You say that I am a teacher ... and so I am." Thirty- three times in the gospel narratives he accepts this title. The religion that he teaches is the central theme of all his teaching about the Kingdom of God and the Kingdom of Heaven. The one purpose of his teaching was that people might be saved by believing in this teaching: "... preach the gospel to every creature. He who believes and is baptised shall be saved." The religion directly revealed to people by Christ was that of God our Father: "My doctrine is not mine, but his who sent me."

Christ claimed that his religion must be embraced by all people (to be saved).

"Go, into the whole world and preach the gospel to every creature. He who believes and is baptised shall be saved, but he who does not believe shall be condemned."

Christ claimed to be the natural Son of God (and therefore to be of the divine nature of God). When the apostle, Peter, proclaimed him to be "The Christ, the Son of the living God," Christ solemnly declared that Peter was "blessed … because flesh and blood have not revealed this to thee, but my Father who is in Heaven." Again: "He who does not honour the Son, does not honour the Father who sent him." His natural sonship must not be mistaken; he is the Son of God, and he is therefore God: "I and the Father are one." To the same point: "Do you not believe that I am in the Father and the Father in me?" This is the substantial unity of the divine persons in God from all eternity: "And now do thou, Father, glorify me with thyself, with the glory that I had with thee before the world existed."

———◆◆◆◆———

There is an urgency in this matter. I must make my decision about Christ carefully and promptly. This is far too important a matter to wait.

These, then, are the claims to be proved.

We can comfortably dismiss the claims of the door-to-door salesperson.

We can wait to find out if the latest style of automobile or washing machine or can opener will stand the test of time.

We can pass up 'the bargain of the century' and still live with ourselves somehow; still think of ourselves as fairly reasonable people.

We can gamble when the stakes are printed on paper.

But, when the stakes are everlasting, when mistakes can be eternally disastrous, when we may be dealing with our God, when there is an unqualified and all-important must to be considered …

A sound mind will put away the calculator or computer which determine the laws of chance. This is no gamble; there is no fall of dice, no cut of the cards to prove a person right or wrong.

Gambling here (on the contents of a water jar as against the claims of Christ) makes less of an appeal to reason than curling up before the fireplace to play 'Russian Roulette'.

Chance plays no part when we are dealing with God.

With such a basic sanity a person must put to the test the claims of Jesus of Galilee.

There is no deferring the all-important decision, when next year may be too late. Next month or even next week may find the brief summary of your life – a name and two dates –

written on a stone over a rising mound of earth … your grave.

In dealing with God, nothing is left to chance.

So, with a purpose and a determination as fixed as the mountains, we must consider the claims and the demands of Christ.

We must decide whether or not we are dealing with God.

"Whoever shall believe in me … the same shall be saved!"

"Whoever does not believe in me … the same shall be condemned!"

Oh no, my soul, this is not a simple matter.

Chapter 3

The Blind See and the Deaf Hear

The case for Christ's divinity, the substantiation of his own profession that he is God, could well be rested with the persuasion of the prophecies which heralded his coming. Such prophecies are obviously and totally beyond human resource, and so thoroughly genuine in their religious implications that they must be taken as the divine corroboration and approval of the words and the works of Christ. But over and above such a persuasion, Christ himself leaves no doubt. Over and over again he repeats his profession that he is the Son of God, that he has the same divine nature as his Father:

"All things which the Father has are mine."

And over and over again this profession is confirmed by miraculous power. A true miracle, one which is beyond suspicion, is an extraordinary intervention of God into the affairs of this world. It is a mark of God's approval, when the miracle is implored as a standard and motive for credence, since it is entirely reasonable to presume that God would not thus intervene to establish error or falsehood. It is entirely reasonable to presume that God's power would not be

65

in the hands of one whose mouth uttered lies. The life of Jesus is a pattern of the power of God. Omnipotence flashed from his finger tips and resided in his softly spoken words. But, for all the many proofs that Christ gave of his divinity, the culmination of his own proof lies in the astounding and unique miracle of his life: his resurrection from the dead.

———◆◈◆———

The miracles of Jesus have two sides. They reveal the tender compassion that he felt for the sick and the suffering, and the great power that faith has with God. Not a less significant side is the probative aspect of miracles. When the imprisoned John the Baptist sent his disciples to find out if the man everyone was talking about was the Christ, Jesus gave those disciples one credential: The blind see, the lame walk, the lepers are cleansed, the deaf hear, the dead rise and the poor have the gospel preached to them.

St Matthew tells us in his gospel narrative how the man who came to announce Jesus of Galilee, one John the Baptist, was imprisoned by an arrogant power, called Herod Antipas, for stirring up the muddy waters of this ruler's conscience, for daring to suggest that there was in the world a power greater than the power of Rome, which he wielded in a limited sort of way.

Herod was a law unto himself.

It is fateful to suggest to such a man that he

cannot lawfully steal his brother's wife. This was the 'suggestion' of the bold Baptist.

No doubt (Herod thought) after this crazed hermit had cooled his heels in a dank dungeon, his enthusiasm for righteousness would settle like the dust after an April rain.

Of course, it was otherwise. The lustful tetrarch eventually discovered that the fire in this man would not be so easily extinguished. But there were shows in the arena to be watched; spicy, tart wines to be sipped; hundreds of slaves to be whipped; and so, not much thought could be wasted on this bearded fanatic, now safely behind the indestructible walls of a Herodian prison.

The kindly rays of the sun were well shut out of that cell which John occupied, but rumours find their way around corners, through iron gratings, and even through the barricades of prisons.

And so, one day, the word seeped through. There was a man in the area who was doing some very unusual things, and his words were even more unusual. He spoke and it was difficult to challenge his authority. He said he was the Christ, the Son of God.

There was exhilaration in John's aching bones at the very thought, and he whispered a question into a friendly ear.

It was the same question you or I would have asked.

It was the same question we are asking ourselves at this very moment. "Are you he who is to come or shall we look for another?"

And so, while Jesus was moving from town to town, always at his work of preaching, he was confronted one day by the messengers of John, and John's question was put to him.

Now this question was not as innocuous as we might think at first ... not just thirteen words which could be answered once and for all in a single word.

The answer would be just as significant to John as it is to you and me. A simple 'yes' would not be enough. The fearless man in King Herod's prison wanted more than this. You and I are looking for more than this.

John knew the prophecies of the Old Testament very well. He knew the vast importance of this question. He knew that if this man was really the Son of God, really the Messiah, then the answer would be a proof, not a simple, cheaply made assertion.

Today we might put it this way: the question was loaded.

There is a theory that John himself knew it was the Christ. The proof was asked not for himself, but for his followers who would bring the question to Jesus.

But it is true that without confidence that this was the Christ, John could not have borne the stale and damp prison air with a singing heart any more than you or I can bear the four walls of our lives.

But if this is the Christ, then for John and for you and me it is enough!

We might, therefore, say that the answer to John's question is the answer to ours.

"And Jesus answering said to them: Go and report to John what you have heard and seen. The blind see, the lame walk, the lepers are cleansed and the deaf hear. The dead rise and the poor have the gospel preached to them!"

———◆◆◆◆———

The significance of this answer and of the miracles of Christ is clear if we understand the meaning, nature, and proving force of miracles in themselves. If Christ claims to be God, then we may very rightly expect him to do what only God can do. Miracles, by their very nature, only God (or someone acting in the name of God) can do.

Here is an answer fraught with meaning; with a meaning that the disciples of John could grasp, that you and I can grasp.

If someone boasts that they are strong, then they must be prepared to do the things that only a strong person can do.

If someone claims to be a genius, then they have to do the things that only a genius can do so as to prove the claim.

If a man says that he is God ... then he must do those things that only God can do.

But ... what can only God do?

The answer is not easy. Be patient.

We live in a world of laws ... laws which we have not made, and which we cannot deny or surpass. Every drop of water in the ocean, every grain of sand on the beach, every autumn leaf that flutters and spins to the ground is subject to laws.

Every body, gaseous, liquid, or solid, observes laws. Scientists would certainly have to find another occupation if the matter they worked with operated by a different set of laws each time they looked through their microscopes or worked with their cyclotrons.

Without these laws, doctors could not discover cures, engineers could not build roads, and teachers could not teach, for there would be nothing to be learned.

We are introduced to these laws from birth.

In the baby's first wail a law is at work.

The first time a child falls or drops a spoon they learn a new lesson, a new law.

A little boy puts his hands into the filled sink, and water runs over the sides onto the floor: at least one law will be learned.

The child looks up at the stars and wonders what holds them up there ... wonders why the sun and the moon do not come crashing down upon the earth ... wonders whatever happened to that skinned knee he had two weeks ago.

And what the child comes to accept as the ordinary course of events is really a set of laws.

Every nature has its laws. And despite the infinite number and minute detail of these laws, there is not a single law court, because there are no violations, no exceptions to these laws! Except ...

Except when the blind man suddenly sees, the lame person suddenly throws away his crutches, or the paralysed man arises from his bed and walks.

Except when the hideous body of the leper is cleansed ...

Except when the deaf hear, the dead rise ... and the poor have the Gospel preached to them!

To understand these laws in detail is impossible.

But to know their origin is not so difficult.

The principles of the first steam engine were determined by the man who made the first steam engine.

It is simple enough.

The laws of the solar system, the skies, the earth, and people are likewise determined by their maker.

... Once more, in the silence of our reasoning ... we find ourselves at the feet of God; God, who made all things; the skies and the earth, the forests and the meadows, the soul and the heart of man.

If, then, we see before our eyes a true and real and undeniable exception to these laws, we know that we have encountered a power beyond the realm of nature, a preternatural power:

An angel, a devil, or God.

But even the brightest of angels ... the darkest of devils ... they know the power of God, the power of God's law. They can do only what God permits them to do.

The angels, the more than eager servants of their creator, are forever doing his will and his work.

But, ah! There is the devil, forever after his own will and his own work; forever trying to bring the darkness and confusion of his home upon the suburbs of humanity.

He can catch the eye, stir wonder in the mind; enter where all is tranquil and leave with all things stormy.

The devil can take the mind of a person up to the mountain tops, offer to make the world at their feet their plaything.

The only thought of the devil is: to deceive ... to put the ring of many promises through the nose of the person who is not alert and lead them around like the saddest of brute beasts.

He cunningly sings the thrush's song, but when the careless nature lover goes to find the source of melody, it is a panther of lust that leaps from the branches.

This very cunning of the devil leaves a question, does it not? When blind eyes see and deaf ears hear, and cures are effected ... there is a doubt. Have we felt the touch of God's hand? Or is it the song of the thrush?

The puzzle is not without a solution.

At least this much is certain:

> When the blind behold the world of colour and shapes, when the blocked channels of hearing are opened again to the sweetest music of sound, when the bodies of the dead walk again ... because one who is holy has called upon God or called upon the powers in himself because he is God ...

> There is no place for mystery.

If God, who is enamoured of the souls of men and women, could hear the prayer of a loved one, and allow the devil to lead that loved one astray, into the endless mazes of error, then:

> There would be one name only for God: Deceiver.

But God, we know, does not, God cannot deceive!

Deception is as foreign to the nature of God as truth is to the father of all lies, the devil.

> External phenomena which seem to be of a mira-

culous nature must be judged carefully; must be judged by the circumstances that surround the phenomena: what has gone before, the phenomena themselves, and the effects they produce. A miracle is good and holy in its beginning, middle, and end.

There is an old adage: *Circumstances* speak.

Applied to the matter at hand, we might say that when the circumstances are the fragrance of holiness and a devout prayer to our Father in heaven, then we can be sure: It is the hand of God that does these things.

When the circumstances are the black billows of a sulphurous smoke, a selfish motive, dishonesty or pretence in any form, God is not there.

This the Jewish people knew twenty centuries ago: "he casts out devils in the name of Beelzebub."

So it was tremendously significant that Jesus of Galilee should have challenged the scorning and accusing Pharisees:

"Which of you can accuse me of sin?"

In the long record of human opinions, no one has ever rightfully accused this Jesus of depravity. People have denied his claims; accused him of being a gullible soul. Others have honoured him with the insult of "A mere but benign Socrates of Religion".

But the charge and the challenge will be forever unacceptable: "Which of you can accuse me of sin?"

74

When the word of such a person opens eyes and ears, brings forth people from the dead, cures the dying, and cleanses the leper, there is only one thing for the reasonable person to admit: This was the power of God.

When the Baptist's disciples brought back the answer of Christ, John knew the meaning: Eyes must be closed to avoid the conclusion.

It is the bedrock reality upon which someone stands, when they confess faith in: "… Jesus, the Christ, God's only Son, our Lord."

Words will never be as eloquent as works. Jesus knew that. You and I know that. And the florist who insists that we 'Say it with flowers' also knows it.

And so the life of Jesus of Galilee is a wealth and a welter of wonders. The power of God flashes out time and time again. Jesus never gave a more eloquent proof of the Godhead than in himself.

Here was the claim to be God … here was the power of God: At most unexpected times. In most unexpected places. Water becomes wine … a leper is made clean … an empty net suddenly bursts with a haul of fish … a man walks on the water … five loaves and two fish feed a multitude … a fig tree withers … and a man takes off the wrappings of death.

This is not a mere biography. This is a study of the power of God!

> A digression on the power of God! Another aspect of this power: trust and confidence in the God to whom this power belongs.

How often we forget that awesome power.

We labour and we fret. We long to fill our barns and our water jars; each night we say 'good night' to a school of well-cultivated worries, and we know that we will meet them again in the morning and live with them always.

We will be forever bothered and eaten away by these parasites as long as we forget: An almighty hand thrust into our lives. An almighty hand in our hand. An almighty source of strength at our side. A hand raised over our lives that was once raised over the turbulent waters of Genesareth and over the leper at Capharnaum.

Things go wrong. Sickness strikes, debts pile up.

Our hearts grow weary and sick. And we forget the voice (of God) that once told us: "Come to me, all you who labour and are heavily burdened, and I will refresh you."

We forget that the best way to know the tender and curing touch of God is to be sick.

———◆◈◆———

Having considered something of the nature and purpose of the miraculous, we proceed now to a consideration of some of the miracles that Jesus performed. The first such miracle which we will take up is the cure of the paralytic at Capharnaum.

The first three of the four original biographers of Jesus tell us of the following incident. It occurred in a small village called Capharnaum, towards the north of Galilee, just off Genesareth or the Sea of Galilee.

The course of his travels had brought Jesus away from his own town, and now he had decided to return.

It was not long before word of his arrival had made the rounds and the people of Capharnaum were gathering together to hear him speak.

On one such occasion, a young paralytic was carried by four friends to the house where Jesus was speaking. These four men were not only well trained but apparently quite determined.

When it was clear that entrance through one of the ordinary doors was impossible because of the bulging crowds, these four friends carried the paralysed man up onto the roof. There they made an opening, and lowered the helpless figure down until he rested at the feet of Jesus.

The young man on the cot lay still and helpless, and no doubt he was worried that this unusual entrance would offend Jesus who had been speaking.

But the heart of Jesus was magnetised by such scenes of suffering. Without invitation (though the young man was obviously being brought to put his powers to the test), he advanced slightly, bent over the cot, and looked down upon the face of this boy.

A tender sympathy was written on his striking features.

The youth looked up and saw him standing there ... he was used to pitying glances, looks of sympathy ... but there was something very different ... strangely different ... in the spell of that countenance.

Here was power and majesty and yet extreme tenderness looking down upon him.

Words would not come.

And then Jesus said to the boy: "Take courage, son; thy sins are forgiven thee." (This did something rather obvious to that crowded room.)

Eyebrows lifted; ears strained as though they had not heard correctly. Eyes widened and stared; and in the shock of such surprise a man at the far wall sent an impulsive but communicative elbow into the ribs of the person next to him.

The words seemed to hang on the now silent air: "Thy sins are forgiven thee."

Later Jesus would commission his apostles to the merciful work of forgiveness of sins in his name. But until that historic moment ... until he would himself declare: "Whose sins you shall forgive are forgiven them. Whose sins you shall retain are retained" ...

Until that moment, the forgiveness of sins was the exclusive right of God alone.

This was what only God could do: "Thy sins are forgiven thee."

It did not require a penetrating mind to sense the meaning of those words.

He was standing there in the shaft of sunlight that streamed through the opened roof, and he was saying this: he was saying that the power of God was his! He was claiming to be God.

The shock was electric.

"And behold, some of the Scribes said within themselves 'This man blasphemes!'"

"Who can forgive sins, but God alone?" they asked.

And the word they chose – blaspheme – was meant to say this: Here is a mere man who says that he has the power to forgive sins, which power belongs to God alone. This man is saying that he is God.

And, in fact, it would have been the most terrible blasphemy, except for this one thing: he was God.

But the amazement that was to sweep down upon the little room of electrified Jews had not yet reached the peak of its full impact. It had hardly begun.

Jesus had not taken his eyes from the numb and helpless form under his gaze.

And yet with a knowledge that knows whenever a sparrow falls; knows the count of leaves in the summertime; knows each blade of grass and the hearts and thoughts of men, he asked: "Why do you harbour evil thoughts in your hearts?"

There was, of course, no reply.

It is embarrassing and silencing to have your most secret thoughts pulled rudely from the sacred privacy of your mind and laid naked before the eyes of all.

It was just as embarrassing then as now.

Then Jesus put another question: "For, which is easier to say, 'Thy sins are forgiven thee,' or 'arise and walk'?"

There was only a vast and significant silence. Staggering minds faced the conclusion, and anxious hearts sensed a climax.

If the power was in this man to make this helplessly damaged body arise and walk, then it had to be believed that his was the power to say: "Thy sins are forgiven thee."

Their bodies stiffened, their muscles drew taut, and in the silence of expectation, they instinctively leaned forward. Everyone tried at once to shift to a vantage point to have the fullest possible view of the scene.

Then Jesus said: "But that you may know that the Son of Man has power on earth to forgive sins" – (turning to the paralytic, he said) – "Arise, take up thy pallet, and go to thy house!"

All eyes fell and were riveted to the figure lying on the cot, the boy they had all seen carried about for many years, the boy they had pitied … "… and he rose, and went away to his house."

———◆◆◆———

We are told that "when the crowds saw it, they were struck with fear, and glorified God…."

So was it always with Jesus of Galilee … if people would but hear him, if people would only let him: he would cause them to give glory to God.

When the powers of evil are at work, the fruit of that work is an evil fruit; people do not fall on their knees and glorify God; they become monsters of lust and passion, and the glory of God is not on their tongues, nor in their hearts.

———◆◆◆———

We do not hear again of the young man who came before the merciful glance of Jesus in such an unusual way. He merely "arose and went away to his house," as he was told to.

Still, we can be sure of this:

He never forgot the power in that face which had looked down upon him in pity. He never forgot the words: "Thy sins are forgiven thee ... Arise, take up thy pallet, and go to thy house."

Nor can we.

The eyes of the Almighty had viewed that scene ... the eyes that have seen all things from all eternity.

Almighty ears heard the words, the promise and the proof.

Our almighty Father saw his power in the power of his son ... one and the same power ... And received the glory of people.

Had it been otherwise, God would have given the proof of his power to the forces of deception, would have branded as true what could never be true, would have allowed people made to his image and likeness to be lost to the forces of evil and destruction.

Had it been otherwise, had Jesus not been God, then God himself would have been blessing blasphemy.

It could not have been otherwise.

The voice of God had been heard unmistakably: "This is my well-beloved son in whom I am well pleased!"

The second miracle: Jesus restores to life the only son of the widow of Naim: "Young man, I say to thee, arise!"

Naim is a small village at the southern end of Galilee, which nestles at the foot of Mount Tabor.

St Luke tells us of a time when Jesus was passing through this district and encountered a funeral procession.

It happened as Jesus and his disciples approached the gates of the town. From a distance they had heard mournful cries of the professional wailers, a traditional part of funeral rites in those days in that place.

As the procession came into sight, Jesus and the disciples politely and silently stepped to the side of the road.

The bier of death was weighted with the body of a youth who had died with all of life before him. There was a unique sadness in the sight: the sadness of a flower that is plucked too soon.

Sadder still was the sight of the frail woman who walked behind the bier, for, as St Luke tells us, she was a widow, and this dead boy had been her only son; had been the centre of all her dreams and hopes; had been her whole life.

Death had robbed her of that life, those dreams and hopes. She knew now what a deep thing grief can be; she knew now how death could be wonderfully enviable, when there is nothing to live for. She knew how fiercely the human heart can ache.

No human heart could have witnessed that scene without experiencing a sharp stab of sympathy ...

Much less the divine heart of Jesus of Galilee.

And so, the procession of death was unexpectedly interrupted, as a stranger from the side of the road approached the anguish-laden widow.

We are told that his first words were what you or I might have said to the lady: "... Do not cry."

That was all he said.

Simply: "Do not cry."

The wailing had stopped. One could not tell how long it would be before this stranger with runaway emotions would recover himself and get off the road. There was still quite a walk to the cemetery, and those carrying the boy's coffin were already arm-sore.

So it was an impatient glance that the party of mourners fixed upon Jesus, in their hurry 'to get it over with'.

But Jesus, turning, "went up and touched the stretcher; and the bearers stood still, and he said: 'Young man, I say to thee, arise!'"

A sudden realisation came clear to those who stood by. It was obvious, once you thought about it: this poor man was insane! Of course he was! No one in his right mind would dare to stalk boldly through such a procession, interrupting the last wails of regret that would be sounded through the streets of Naim for this boy.

But it was not perfectly clear that the man was demented, until this: until he walked over to the lifeless and cold form and said: "I say to thee, arise!"

These were the things they thought. And then ...

Then, "He who was dead, sat up, and began to speak...."

The imagination delights in picturing the scene that must have followed. St Luke says only this: "And he gave him to his mother."

As to the impatient members of the procession, it was the same result as before: "But fear seized upon all, and they began to glorify God, saying ... God has visited his people!"

"God has visited his people." How well you reasoned, little band of mourners in ancient Naim.

Dear widow of Naim: Did you ever forget the comforting hand that supported you in the throes of your grief? If you had lived a thousand years could you have ever forgotten the depth and strength and consoling power in the words: "Do not cry"? Did you ever dream back to the wonderful moment? Did you see that face? Did you bless that hand which gave your only son back to you?

Did you hear that voice in the roar of the surf and sweep of the winds? It was there. Did you see that hand in the starlit sky? Did you see it in the height of the hills or in the delicate veins of a leaf turning gold? It was there. Did you feel the power and strength of that man in every subsequent moment of your life? Dear widow, it was there. Twice had he given you that much loved son. For his was the power that once caused life in your womb ... And his was the power that gave that life back to your embrace, back to your aching heart, just outside the gates of Naim.

The same power then.

The same power now ... and always: The power of God.

Some personal reflections on the miracles of Christ: the meaning and importance of these miracles to me. The power and tenderness of God in my life.

Such scenes leave the heart impressed and even glowing, but what is more important: they weigh the mind with a conviction. A man claims to be sent from God, claims to be God. And the power of God thunders in his words; it streams from his hands.

Even the saltiest of a 'salt-barrel' generation must say in their heart, as a Roman Centurion had said centuries before, when he opened the side of Christ with a lance: "This was indeed the Son of God."

<hr/>

Supposing a person does believe ... supposing a person does believe that once there lived on earth a man called Jesus of Galilee. He said he was sent from God to be a teacher of people ... he said he was God, and he proved his claim beyond all shadow of doubt. He did the things which only God can do.

> Might I ask: so what? Is Jacob's Well of any importance today? What do Capharnaum and Naim mean to me?
>
> Me, a banker on Wall Street?
>
> Me, an underpaid and under-appreciated checkout operator, a real first-class flunkey?
>
> Me, the latest rage of stage, screen and TV?
>
> Me, the most popular person on the campus?
>
> Me, the wretched little nobody with hungry kids and a drunken husband?
>
> Me, the old man who has had his hour on the stage, and is ready for oblivion?
>
> Me, a sweaty and grimy factory worker whose ironic contribution to civilisation is driving a forklift truck?

What does Jacob's Well, Capharnaum, Naim mean to me?

What does it mean to me, today, that God visited his earth and his people in the distant and shadowy past?

What good is that now to the poor 'sucker' who hasn't got a shirt to cover his back, or food to fill his stomach?

Pretty thoughts about God's tenderness won't heat an apartment filled with starving children and crawling rats.

It won't help the desperately hungry and the homeless to know of Naim. And the stuffy, over-weight rich won't be thrilled to the marrow to hear that the Messiah once put in an appearance at Jacob's Well in Samaria.

So what? you ask, as millions have asked before you: So what?

So this perhaps:

The Messiah was not only in Capharnaum and Naim and at Jacob's Well. His power was not only there for the unsightly leper, the blind, and the paralysed.

His words were meant to be the food and the text of life, not only for the Jewish people twenty forgotten centuries ago.

He does not run out of mercy or 'living water' after three years of public life, or three thousand years. Whatever is his is limitless.

The rewards he promised and the pains he threatened were not just for then but for always.

The 'little ones' whom he would guard and pursue with a tender and fatherly love were not enclosed within the fence of one nation or one age.

The Messiah is waiting at your door, even where there is no knob ... even if you have no house.

The power that once streamed from his almighty hands, the power of Naim and Capharnaum is yours, if only you will put your hand into his.

The teaching of Christ is not outmoded like grandmother's book of table manners. It is for life. Yes, your life, here and now.

His teaching is for all people, everywhere, at all times.

Believe this, if you can: You are Christ's 'little ones', the 'little one' that Christ loves so tenderly. Believe in him and trust in his love for you.

Now follow this carefully:

This is what Capharnaum and Naim and Jacob's Well mean to you.

If Christ's claims were true ...

If he is God ...

Then his is an infinite knowledge ...

He knew and he knows all things. In his divine mind all things are known in one, eternal now.

At once he sees the sparrow that fell yesterday, the lily that will blossom tomorrow.

If you accept these things ... there is no way around it

... this was the fact: At Jacob's Well, at Naim,

on the Sea of Galilee, in Capharnaum, and on Mount Calvary …

He was thinking of you.

He was thinking of you in your dingy office, in your sweaty factory, in the deep, dark coal mine where you disembowel the earth of her riches, in your mansion, in your apartment; in your humble hut; wherever you work, wherever you live, wherever you are.

He was thinking of your sorrows and worries. He was thinking of you in the gnawing pains of your loneliness … in the bottomless sensitivities of your human heart.

But the most beautiful thing is this: he loves you. From all eternity he has loved you, wanted you, wanted to possess and be possessed by you. He has wanted to be wanted by you.

You may not believe this … now. But someday you will understand very clearly. This you can believe right now (perhaps it is the easiest thing for you to believe) – one day you will die. The thin veil that separates this life from eternity will be snatched away, as though it were a thin silk scarf.

Then you will see … with such a terrible clarity.

Will this realisation then come as a painful one? Will you be torn apart with grief that you missed the point for such a long time?

Consolation waits for you, now, at your

doorstep. Go to the door of your life, and let Christ in. Go to him because you need him. Go to him because you want to return his love. Go and rest in the power of Capharnaum and Naim.

Perhaps we do not know what Christ means today because the door of our lives is closed tightly ... or because we are blithely unaware that he is waiting to enter our lives and mean everything to us.

> The third miracle: Jesus raises Lazarus from the dead. "I am the resurrection and the life. He who believes in me, even if he die, shall live. And whoever lives and believes in me, shall never die."

Let us go back again ... this time to an incident in the life of Jesus, related by St John. (Jesus knew that someday you would read or hear of this incident. If nowhere else, then here in these lines ... in this book. It is true that as God, in his divine mind he knew all things. Even in Bethany, over nineteen centuries ago, back in a drafty little cottage by the brook of Cedron where this incident takes its setting [Do not be surprised] ... you were there. You were there in the eye and focus of his thought. You were there in the vast, warm love of his heart. In his every action and word, he was thinking of you.)

Bethany was a little village in northern Judea, not many miles from Jerusalem, at the side of the brook of Cedron.

In little Bethany, there lay dying a man named Lazarus.

As death hovered on silent wings over this man, his grieving sisters, Mary and Martha, sent an urgent message of need to Jesus, whom they had known and loved. (Maybe sometime in the past you, too, have sent such a message ... to a doctor, or a mother or father, to come quickly to a dying loved one. If so you will be able to understand the anxiety in the hearts of these women. You will know what it is to need someone ... badly.)

You know perhaps how your heart would have reacted to the message which Jesus returned to Mary and Martha. It was hardly to be expected.

They wrote: "Lord, your dear friend is sick!"

And he said simply: "This sickness is not unto death, but for the glory of God, that through it the Son of God may be glorified."

You or I would have twisted and scraped the words for meaning, for some possible, consoling meaning.

We would have read it again and again: "This sickness is not unto death."

———◆◆◆◆◆———

St John tells us that for two days afterwards Jesus stayed in the region of the Jordan.

Why did he wait?

And then when the two days had passed – although there had been no message of any kind – he, who knew all things, knew: Lazarus had died!

Imagine the grief of Mary and Martha. He to whom they had learned to turn in every grief, whose power they had seen so clearly to be the power of God; he who had calmed the wind and the waves, he had promised that this sickness would not bring death. But now, one thing was certain: Lazarus was dead.

We might wonder if it wasn't nearly a double death. How easily the love and faith of the sisters might have died with their good brother, in the darkness of that night of trial.

"Then afterwards he said to his disciples, 'Let us go again into Judea.'"

The disciples protested. The Jews had attempted to stone him in Judea. He could not return now. It would be his death.

But his eye was not on himself. His eye was on 'his little one'.

"Lazarus, our friend, sleeps," he said.

"Sleeps?" That was a puzzling thought. The reaction of the disciples is convincingly normal. With the simplicity of a child, they answered: "If he sleeps, he will be safe."

"So then Jesus said to them plainly, 'Lazarus is dead.'"

There was a sudden and reverent hush; an "Oh!" that only the inmost heart hears and feels.

Then Jesus added "... and I rejoice on your account that I was not there that you may believe. But let us go to him." (Let us not forget that we too are with Jesus, in his thoughts. Let us not forget that he rejoiced on our account also: that we might believe.)

Then the disciple, Thomas, who had learned well and believed deeply in the blessedness after death of which Jesus had spoken, began to think earnestly about: That reward which "eye hath not seen, nor ear heard ..."

Now Thomas was convinced that a return to Judea would not only mean death for Christ, but also for those who walked at his side.

By this time, his reflections had swept Thomas up to a gratifying loyalty and heroism: "Let us go also that we may die with him."

If Jesus was to die, Thomas would perish with him – a single eye and a faithful heart.

And so the little band departed for Bethany.

Jesus knew all the while that someday they, too, would rejoice that he had not been there when Lazarus had died. For in some distant day those disciples would suffer terribly for him, and they would need the strength that the experience soon to be theirs would afford.

Word that he was coming had meanwhile passed before him over the road that leads to

Bethany, and so the ever faithful Martha went out to meet Jesus.

As he went along, he saw her approach. His divine eyes looked into her heart. He saw there an indestructible faith ... faith of steel. He knew that her words would be:

"If you had been here Lord my brother would not have died."

He saw the hope that still burned brightly in her heart and on her quivering lips: "But I know that even now God will give you whatever you ask for."

And Jesus answered: "Your brother will rise to life."

But Martha misunderstood his meaning: "I know that he will rise to life, on the last day."

Then Jesus looked sympathetically into those eyes reddened with weeping, and glistening now with fresh tears ... into that face disarrayed by grief but radiant with faith, and he whispered softly: "I am the resurrection and the life; those who believe in me, shall live even if they die; and those who believe in me, will never die.

Do you believe this?"

Her answer was perfect. It must have been a warmth to the heart of Jesus: "Yes, Lord, I believe that you are the Christ, the Son of God, who has come into this world."

This is the faith that moves mountains ... the faith that brings the dead back to life again.

"I am the resurrection and the life. He who believes in me, even if he die, shall live; and whoever lives and believes in me, shall never die!" How many aching heads and hearts would lean upon the soft comfort in those words ... In dimly lit rooms where an angel of death is awaited in silence ... In the hearts of many a mother and father told of the death of their son on some distant battlefield, or buried under the billows of the ocean tide ...

By the side of a cemetery plot where a dear one lies at rest ... In the painfully great voids of life left by the visitation of death:

Places never to be filled again.
Voices no longer heard.
The disappearance of a comforting hand and a
    consoling smile.

In all these, one consolation: "I am the resurrection and 'the life'!"

For these words to Martha were a new comfort. Death was proclaimed a door ... a beginning ... a birth ... a springtime.

The unbearable sting is gone forever.

The world will still seem to wobble and fall when death comes to steal a piece of the human heart.

War Department communications will never cease to wring the hearts of mothers and fathers with terrible grief in times of war.

Human hearts will continue to ache and ache

... But, the grief, the sorrow and the ache will not be filled with despair.

There is a comfort now ... a new consolation ... a new hope: "I am the resurrection and the life!"

It is the hope in the heart of every person going into battle.

The hope of the world riding on sinking ships and crashing planes.

The hope within the heart when the doctor places all in God's hands.

The hope that will someday be yours and mine in our last moments.

The hope of every person who believes in him. "I am the resurrection and the life. He who believes in me, even if he die, shall live!"

———◆◈◆———

After his arrival, Mary and Martha took Jesus to the tomb of Lazarus, who was four days dead.

Then, we read three words we must never forget: "And Jesus wept."

What was the meaning of these tears? Did they stand for the weakness of man? Uncontrollable floods of emotion which break over all men at times? Did the heart of Christ give way under the weight of grief?

Whenever we reach for an explanation about these tears, we always return empty handed.

There seems to be only one answer: Jesus

wept that you might know, that Mary and Martha might know, that I might know: An infinite sympathy ... a heart that would always have tears for human grief ... an infinite understanding of human sorrow and the human heart.

The love of Christ will always and everywhere bend over the wounds of humanity: the torn flesh and the torn hearts.

The tears that fell from the eyes of Jesus, and coursed down his cheeks in an unexpected show of emotion are a reminder of that love and sympathy and understanding which God will always have for people.

Too often, we forget those tears. We exile ourselves from that belief and comfort which alone can assuage our grief and loneliness: the belief that someone is there in the darkness of sorrow ... the comfort of knowing that he wishes only to console.

It seems quite certain that we will never feel abandoned in our grief, or alone in our sorrow, if we just remember three words: "And Jesus wept."

Without some realisation of God's compassion, the world becomes a world of thorns and bramble, because there is always a time when the words of sympathy that others offer are distant, unfeeling and of no comfort. And there are times when the words of others are not offered.

There should never be a time when we are

not able to find comfort and strength in the eyes of Jesus, filled with tears; in the vision of God's head bowed in sorrow.

Lazarus was dead.

———————

Lazarus had been laid in a cave, and a stone stood guard at the entrance.

And so it was that Jesus said: "Take away the stone."

We can easily imagine the concern and regret that swept up into the face of Martha, as she said: "Lord, by this time he is already decayed, for he is dead four days."

Christ's answer gave the first bright hint that the power of God was to break forth once more, and that the grief in Bethany would be banished: "Have I not told you," he said quietly, "that if you believe you shall see the glory of God?"

"They therefore removed the stone."

"And Jesus, raising his eyes, said, 'Father, I give you thanks that you have heard me; but because of the people who stand round, I spoke, that they may believe that you have sent me.'"

The lowering clouds of doubt are about to be parted by power and the light of God is about to stream down upon people.

Always and everywhere Christ asks people for the complete gift of their hearts. He asks them to suffer for him. He asks for a service of sacrifice.

He demands from each of us a love greater than that which we feel for our very own mother and father. He asks of some a trust and a faith till the last drop of blood has been poured out. He asks people to endure crosses and fires and the fangs of lions for his sake ... to be ground into the dust for him.

And so he wanted to prove his right to make these demands. He knew much better than we that it is hard to bleed, hard to endure, hard to die. People would have proof that to bleed, endure, and die for him is a glorious thing and not a sad delusion.

So he would offer a proof that people could never deny. A proof that death for his sake means life and glory and reward, and satiety for the thousand thirsts of the heart. For, knowing all things, he knew: People do not die for words.

Consequently, "When he had said this, he cried out with a loud voice: 'Lazarus, come out!' "

The die was cast.

For the little group that stood at the mouth of that cave, in which Lazarus had rested for four days, the decision about Jesus of Galilee was at a critical point.

If he is God, then all doubt will be carried away by the evening winds in Bethany, and human eyes will see what is humanly impossible. But if life does not stir in that little cave of death, then all his claims and all the demands he asks of people must be erased from human memory. The book will be closed once and for all. Jesus of Galilee will be just one of the many impostors to appear in our history books.

"And at once he who had been dead came forth, bound feet and hands with wrappings, and his face was tied up with a cloth."

<hr/>

This was to be one of the last legacies of Jesus, for St John tells us that when the news came to the ears of the already anxious Pharisees, it set off a fuse of panic and frenzy. "If we let him alone as he is, all will believe in him, and the Romans will come and take away both our place and our nation."

So it was. The picture of the angry face of Rome sent chills through these poor, bloodless men, and they weakly determined that it was expedient to barter truth for Roman complacency. The supreme reward: the smile of Rome. What would it profit them: to gain the whole world, but suffer the loss of the smile of Rome?

Had these poor men, the Pharisees, but known. Had they been able to look forward, as you and I can look back, and see the once great colossus of the Roman Empire; see it as a sleeping giant whose angry power has long since been forgotten; lying in the dust of time, harmlessly dead; mere brittle bones for the excavator and historian.

Had they been able to see the growth and harvest of that seed planted in Naim and Capharnaum and Bethany; the devotion that would creep like a wild vine over the face of the earth, watered by the blood of a million martyrs; nurtured from the wounds of persecution, ever growing, spreading and reaching out to the four corners of the earth, over the hills and valleys of two thousand years...

Had their eyes been able to see this, the line that follows in St John would certainly have been left unwritten: "So from that day forth their plan was to put him to death!"

But just as the Pharisees would lament, "Behold, the entire world has gone after him!" and eventually put Jesus to death on the cross of disgrace, so Lazarus, too, according to their plans, would pay with the life that had just been restored to him.

It is not surprising.

A living, walking proof of the power of Jesus was a dangerous thing.

It would be a betraying tolerance and an insult to the glorious empire of Rome to allow such a man to walk the streets as he pleased, all the while reminding people that there was in this world a power much greater than Rome.

This man, Lazarus, was lighting too many

fires of enthusiasm, and these were not healthy for the men upon whom Rome had laid the fearsome hand of her trust.

This Lazarus was a reminder; a proof in flesh and bones. His very presence was like a message in the sky: "I am the resurrection and the life!"

It was not to be tolerated.

———◆◆◆———

The whole message of Jesus, his claims, his demands, walked about in the person of this living confirmation. They walked about in the market place and in the temple. The people who had all paid their last respects to Lazarus were now paying another kind of respect to him who had called Lazarus from the dead. In fact, they were quite carried away and wanted to hear all they could about this Jesus of Galilee.

For the Pharisees this was dreadful. The alarm had been sounded. This was a challenge that could be met only by death.

And so, one day, according to tradition, Lazarus appeared no more.

———◆◆◆———

But Lazarus was not unique. If the days of miracles are not over, neither are the days of Lazaruses. Would it be an overstatement to say that the world is filled with Lazaruses? Fires … that will not go out.

Today Lazaruses are burning brightly behind and beneath what is left of communism. They burn in distant and uncivilised lands; in our big cities and our sprawling farm lands. They burn in factories, offices and supermarkets. They burn on the highways of this twentieth century.

These are the witnesses and proofs of the power of God!

These people are veins of life running through the body of humanity, a humanity which is sick with a thousand ills.

Men and women and little children whose souls are alive with the love and faith of Mary and Martha, alive with love and enthusiasm for Christ.

Somewhere in the life of each of us there is a Lazarus, a reminder that God is all-powerful, all-merciful.

Wherever there is a life lived for Jesus alone, there is a Lazarus. A living proof of God's goodness and power, walking the streets of our lives, pregnant with hope, and radiantly confident with the confidence of one promise: "I am the resurrection and the life!"

Are we not, in another sense, all of us Lazarus … we have all received life from the same almighty will that determined to cry, "Lazarus, come forth!"

Just as a charred ruin stirs images of the flames, and the dawn looks back into the darkness, so each spark of life in every person – the propulsion of infinitely numerous thoughts and desires from his or her mind and will … the recoil of joy at a morning in spring … the innocent ecstasy in the face of a happy child … and even the pain in a person's heart – recall the flame of God.

For life in each person is a Lazarus. A reminder of the voice once heard in Bethany: "I am the resurrection and the life. He who believes in me, even if he die, shall live; and whoever lives and believes in me, shall never die!"

And we, too, must rejoice that he was not there … that Lazarus had actually died … that we, too, might believe.

> The culmination of Christ's proof that he is God, and the final miracle of our consideration: Jesus raises himself from the dead. "After three days I will rise."

Love is more a thing of deeds than words.

And love in deeds has never reached a higher climax than on a day almost two thousand years ago on a rising hill in Judea called Calvary, the place of crucifixion.

Greater endurance for love has never been written in human blood … here meekness and courage met in one flesh. Strength and tenderness, in magnificent proportions, joined in one man beyond any hope of repetition … in the crucifixion of Jesus of Galilee.

That day has been solemnly laid into the neglected vaults of time, trampled into oblivion by two thousand years of ever changing feet, by two million distracting concerns. The vision has lost its focus. The image is dull.

But if we believe with a consuming belief; if we believe deeply and devoutly and with our whole heart, so deeply that we almost kneel again on Mount Calvary and see the blood-covered body of Christ; if we once look up into the dying eyes of Jesus of Galilee, then we will never forget. The heart will not be in us to dare whisper, even when no one else can hear, "Jesus, you ask too much of me." We will never kneel in the shadow of that cross, and demur: "Jesus, I have now suffered enough for you."

Nor could we think of saying: "I'm sorry I do not have the time or inclination to consider your cause and demands."

Nor could we ever doubt the mercy that God has for people. If we could only believe: "Father, forgive them, for they know not what they do!"

We cannot find any refutation for this kind of mercy. We cannot refute the forgiveness that comes from bleeding lips ... lips quivering with pain ... the pale lips of death.

At three o'clock that afternoon, the voice of Jesus, once laden beyond belief with power, was heard to gasp: "It is finished!"

His head dropped down upon his chest.

Jesus of Galilee was dead.

Humanly speaking, it was the end. It was the final conclusion, humanly speaking. The great finish to a great life had been written with hammer and nails. A spring of mercy and power had been drained to the last drop ... humanly speaking.

The Jewish high priests and the Pharisees were then able to glory in the triumph of the moment.

And the breezes which had carried word of Jesus over the churning waters of the Mediterranean into the very precincts of Rome were cleared now of suspicion and rumour. Even in Rome, this man had caused people to catch their breath, but now breathing was regular and easy ... humanly speaking.

As the darkness of the night settled that evening over Judea, there was obviously a note of finality – even in the heavy hearts of that small group of people who were mourning the blood that was still wet on the rocks of Calvary.

Mourning was mingled with fear in the hearts of the disciples, as they huddled together behind the barred doors of the little cenacle. If the Jews decided to rip out of Judean soil every root and fibre of enthusiasm planted by Jesus, their blood would also redden the soil. To these scared disciples that was a terrifying thought.

So, there was a sense of triumph and a sense of defeat that night in Judea, for: Jesus of Galilee was dead … humanly speaking.

But he had never said that the venture of his life was a human venture. In fact, his insistence had been otherwise. The laws which the human race must obey were thin and brittle bands, which broke apart at his word, and at his touch.

In the transcendence of his godly powers, he had made it very clear that he was outside and above human calculation.

Of him there could be no 'humanly speaking'.

For one thing, when a person is dead – humanly speaking – he or she is dead. There is no return.

But Christ had promised that, after the hammers and nails had done their work, he would, through his own power, walk back through the walls which bar return, and be once more in their midst. Three days he would remain in the land of the dead, by his own prophecy and promise. "For even as Jonah was in the belly of the whale three days and three nights, so will the Son of Man be three days and three nights in the heart of the earth."

But, after those three days and nights, he would return to the 'little ones' whom he had loved. "After I have risen, I will go before you into Galilee."

After Calvary, however, hope was very thin. Hope rested solely in that promise. Three days of hope were the only remnants left after Good Friday, after the cross.

The counterpart of this hope was suspicion and fear. "And on the next day the leaders of the people and the Pharisees came to Pilate, saying: 'Lord, we have recorded that the Seducer said while yet alive: After three days I will rise.' Pilate, therefore, officially ordered the sepulchre to be guarded until the third day."

The power of Naim and Capharnaum was on the one hand trusted, but on the other hand feared.

The final test would be simple; it all hinged on 'an empty tomb'. He had said that by his own power he would rise again.

Now the power of God was on trial, and the verdict would affect the life and destiny of everyone, present and future generations. The hope in the hearts of those who loved him, the fears of those who crucified him, would be settled beyond all question in: an empty tomb.

———◆◆◆———

Among the hearts broken on Mount Calvary was that of one Mary Magdalen.

Mary Magdalen, in worse days and better, was living proof, as we are all living proof, that the human heart was made to love; made to stretch forth long, hungry arms to find love, refusing to be denied.

It is the universal law of the human heart.

When the heart does not fasten God in its embrace, it will lay hold of itself in one of two forms: It will have the single eye of pride … or it will inhabit the ghettos of lust.

But it will not be denied. The human heart will love at any cost.

To understand in a kindly, sympathetic, Christlike light the soul which has been made ugly by sin, one must understand this tremendous impulse in the heart of a person: to love.

Mary Magdalen had been a woman of the streets. No doubt, inside and outside her hearing, she was called cheap, degraded, a 'tramp' by her self-appointed judges who were blind to the problems of the human heart.

Her life had been a dark and lonely night of lust, until the dawn of Jesus of Galilee broke in her life.

It was then, for the first time, that she saw through the mist of her copious tears the pure beauty for which the heart is made. It was then, for the first time, that she read it in the leaves and flowers, heard it in the song of the birds, and saw it in the face of Jesus of Galilee.

Her life opened then with her eyes; her heart felt 'at home' and the deepest instincts of that heart in her knew it and would never doubt: this was the love that she had sought in a million places; these were the waters of life that now washed soothingly over her tiredness.

Her hands were cracked and bleeding from the digging, but she had, in the end, found the treasure she had been seeking all her life.

And she had found this purest of all gifts in the hands she had just beheld, pierced by nails and twisting in pain, against the sky on Mt Calvary.

This was the Mary Magdalen who, in the deepest darkness of the night, came to the tomb of Jesus on the morning of the third day ... blind to every consideration of danger and inconvenience ... blind to everything, perhaps, except love.

Having arrived in the little garden where Jesus had been laid, she saw by the last rays of the moon a thing she had never expected: the stone at the entrance of the cave was removed, and the grave stood open.

The chill of the night air and the shock of this surprise sent a tremor of fear through her, and in an instant she turned back hurriedly over the moonlit road to tell the sleeping apostles of her discovery.

"They have taken the Lord from the tomb, and we do not know where they have laid him," she related breathlessly.

New courage and indignation pounded in

the veins of Peter and John, as they raced to the tomb, only to find: "... the linen cloths lying there, and the handkerchief which had been about his head, not lying with the linen cloths, but folded in a place by itself."

The two apostles, who had loved Jesus with every fibre of their hearts, straightened up and their eyes met. There was no word for there was no need for a word. Each read it clearly and carefully in the smiling face of the other.

A thousand things were now beginning to be clear: All that he had said ... Yet, it was too great a thing to have become clear and certain in a flash. But clarity and certainty had begun to shine forth from those neatly folded cloths.

In the distance the first bird opened its throat in song, but the music in the hearts of the apostles swelled even more beautifully: Jesus had risen!

There was a new and joyous spring in their steps as they anxiously made their way back over the road from the tomb. Their hearts were thundering in their breasts. And the rising of the sun in the east poured its light down upon a new world of hope and rewarded faith.

But behind them (it must have been pure oversight) they left a still sorrowful figure weeping in the shadows of the garden.

Poor Mary Magdalen.

Perhaps you will pause at this place in St

John's Gospel, as often I have, to feel a momentary sorrow for Mary. After all, it had been Mary who, in the terrifying momentum of her overpowering love for Jesus, had run to tell the apostles.

But when the meaning was clear ... When the nicely folded death wrappings announced their solemn message, the apostles had rushed off with brimming hearts without telling Mary, who had waited outside the cave in the shadows of the garden – alone.

When the sun of this tremendous realisation that Jesus had risen broke through to light the worlds of Peter and John, poor Mary was left a solitary figure of grief, alone in the shadows.

But a divine plan was deeply woven into the pattern ... hidden for the moment, but soon to reveal itself most tenderly.

For St John tells us (the same John who had gone off with Peter): "But Mary was standing outside weeping at the tomb. So, as she wept, she stooped down and looked into the tomb, and saw two angels in white sitting, one at the head and one at the feet, where the body of Jesus had been laid ..."

Eyes which have done without sleep and which are misty with tears can be forgiven for not recognising these white figures as being citizens of another world. For it is apparent from the dialogue that Mary did not make this judgement. "Woman, why are you weeping?" "Because they have taken away my Lord, and I do not know where they have laid him." (The mother who has lost a son on some deserted and uncertain battlefield, or under the vast tides of the ocean, will alone fully understand the tears on Mary's cheeks ... the grief in Mary's heart at not knowing where the body of Jesus lay.)

Then again the same question: "Woman, why are you weeping?" But this time the question was put by a man suddenly discovered to be standing in the garden. "Whom do you seek?" he asked.

Mary's heart, tired and worn with grief, was in another world. It was back on the road where she had first seen Jesus; back in the world of joy and forgiveness; back in the days when she beheld him pouring mercy over the sick, giving sight to the blind ... back, too, on Calvary where he died.

If there was an other-worldly light about these figures standing guard in the black tomb, it is hardly surprising that Mary did not see it. It is not surprising that she thought the man in the garden was a caretaker. No wonder she exclaimed: "Sir, if you have removed him, tell me where you have laid him and I will take him away."

The moment had arrived. The sun was at the horizon; but for Mary there was to be no slow-breaking dawn, no early morning. There would suddenly and simply be a gloriously bright world. All the memories of the shadows and the darkness would be forever gone.

It was all the warmth and the brightness of a cloudless high noon, when: "Jesus said to her, 'Mary'!" "Rabboni ... Master!"

How blessed you were, Mary, in the thoughtlessness of Peter and John. Had you read the message of the linen cloths you would now be back in the cenacle describing what you had seen in that early dawn of hope. You would not now be kissing devoutly the once-ghastly wounds of Calvary, now transformed and shining as brightly as the sun.

Yours was a double blessing, Mary. A blessing for yourself and a blessing for us, for in the ecstasy of that early morning, so many years ago, in that tender reunion of which we may now read, there is a new certainty; a new confirmation that our trust and faith are grounded solidly on the immovable rock of Christ's divinity.

Like you, Mary, we know that we have not believed in vain.

In the resurrection of Jesus from the dead there is an undying pledge that someday we too shall rise again. Jesus had promised that there would be a day when he would come on the clouds of heaven; when he would send his angels of judgement to cities and hinterlands of humanity to claim his elect ... to claim those who have loved him.

On his word, we shall rise from the graves in which our bodies shall someday rest ... rise as he did with the scars that the conflict has cost us shining brightly even as his wounds ... we have his word.

Really, Mary Magdalen did not wait alone at the mouth of that sepulchre and tomb. The human race stood with fixed eyes at her side. And the joy that bubbled over in her heart at the sight of him is the same quiet hope which we press to our hearts, knowing that someday the dedication of our lives to him shall bring us that same vision.

Christ, we know, is risen!

Chapter 4

A Kingdom and a Church

We must go back to Christ's life, and make that life living for ourselves, by study and by prayer. At the same time, we must accept Christ as he is now living in this, our day, and in this, our world. Christ spoke often of his Kingdom, not wishing to say from the first that his work of atonement and redemption would include the institution of a new law of the Jews and their temple. The Jewish people, in anxious regard for their own religion, their law and their temple, would certainly have put Christ to death had he been bold and direct from the beginning. It is true that he was their Messiah, but time and human imagination had distorted the descriptions of the prophecies. Instead of the Messiah they had been told by the prophets to expect, they had taken to looking for a temporal, political, and material Messiah. The beatitudes of Christ, which would bless poverty, meekness, and suffering, were hardly a part of their anticipation. Gradually, then, in the face of such preconceptions and prejudices, Christ founded his Church, the living voice of his teaching, the living perpetuation of his mission among people.

Withstanding all the disorders and attacks to which human organisations are subject, his Church has endured the trials and tribulations of twenty centuries, producing for God's world thousands of saints, and growing with an increase which finds explanation only in the favour and protection of almighty God. Christ's Church has for these long years remained steadfast in her protection of his teachings, refusing compromise, refusing to modernise the truths which Christ taught and championed. She has offered the world the countless fruits of her divine enterprise, and she remains confident in her role in the drama of human salvation, because Christ has promised her:

> "I will be with you all days, even unto the consummation of the world."

The sceptic Ernest Renan, once said: "A thousand times more loving, a thousand times more beloved since his death than during the days he passed upon the earth, Jesus Christ has become to such a degree the cornerstone of humanity that to take away his name from the world would be to shake it to its foundations."

And yet …

There will always be Capharnaum … There will always be Naim and Bethany.

118

There will always be an empty tomb, and the neatly folded wrappings of death.

There will always be the sick, the sightless, and the unclean who are given health and vision and cleanliness through words with hidden power; through soft, transforming touches of an almighty hand.

And these will forever be beacons throwing a brilliant light from a tower twenty centuries distant: through the years in an almost endless succession: 1999 ... 2009 ... 2019. .. 2029...

And when the great sound of Gabriel's trumpet startles our distracted human race, on some unknown future day, that light shall be shining just as surely as the sun.

The last person, on that last day, will, if only they choose, read the why and the wherefore by the brilliance of that light of Christ shining out of the ancient past.

The light that was life ... the light that is the light of the world.

Each of us shall someday be ushered from the stage of this life, through the inevitable exit of death and we shall each be judged in that light, judged to be worthy to live eternally in the land of light, or ... destined to the doom and damnation of our choosing.

"For as the lightning comes forth from the east and shines even to the west, so also will the coming of the Son of Man be ... And then will appear the sign of the Son of Man in heaven; and then will all tribes of the earth mourn, and they will see the Son of Man coming upon the clouds of heaven with great power and majesty. And he will send forth his angels with a trumpet and a great sound, and they will gather his elect from the four winds, from one end of the heavens to the other".

And so we must go back, now, back to Capharnaum, to Naim and Bethany ... back to the source of light, and the source of life.

For one who would give his sincere mind to the study of Christ's life and person the way ahead is challenging. It is not easy nor always delightful to study, read, and pray about Christ. But Christ never promised ease in this life. In fact, it is the cross that symbolises Christ. One thing, however, Christ's follower will certainly possess: life eternal.

Despite the lure of the golf course, the tennis club, (not to mention cinema and television) ... despite the fact that the leisure to think and read and pray is not apparent ...

We must make reasonable concessions to demands upon our time, but this, this we must demand: We must demand of ourselves the strength and determination to pray ... to say no without compromising when some new fascination would rob us of the time we have marked off '... for God'.

We must demand of ourselves a promise not to turn back, when the journey back to Christ seems too long or too unrewarding.

We must demand time.

Time is of the essence. Time is to be treasured.

For it takes time to ponder the Gospels, to understand the import and meaning of Christ in our lives, to see the appeal of Christ, to be moved by the persuasions of his proofs.

It takes time and prayer for the heart to feel the thrill of power, the impact and the realisation of the divine; time to know and to live, love, and learn... to find God's comforts.

It is so necessary that we take our tired hearts back to Christ ... that we sit on the hillside and eat bread and fishes with the multitude ... to sit with Christ at Jacob's well in Samaria, and listen to words which promise 'living water' ... to see bandaged Lazarus emerging from his tomb after four days of death ... to live over again these scenes.

We must above all stand at the foot of the cross ... upon which the world was redeemed ... and wait with Mary Magdalen in the garden of resurrection.

We must take up the Gospels then ... read them ... live them ... learn from them ... study them ... and pray over every line.

As you are reading these poor lines, the watch at your wrist or the clock on your kitchen wall is ticking away the seconds. To you these are vital seconds ... seconds not to be wasted.

There is a stranger at your door ... There is a question to be answered.

While it is altogether necessary that we learn about Christ from the Gospels, as he was then, it is equally vital that we meet Christ in our own day as he is now, here and among us. Christ's Kingdom and Christ in his Kingdom are very much a part of our daily living. We turn now to a consideration of the Kingdom of Christ in its historical setting.

At the same time ...

The Kingdom of Christ is not a tower of the past ... fallen. Nor a fire of devout enthusiasm burnt out ... cold ashes. Nor the arc of a flame in the sky ... a meteoric moment.

No, none of these, because: "I will be with you all days, even unto the consummation of the world."

The Kingdom of Christ was then and was there.

But the Kingdom is also now and here.

It will always be even until the consummation of the world, when the love which binds men to Christ becomes an eternal bond; when the Kingdom of time becomes a Kingdom of eternity.

"Do not lay up for yourselves," he said, "treasures on earth, where rust and moth consume, and where thieves break in and steal; but lay up for yourselves treasures in heaven, where neither rust nor moth consumes, nor thieves break in and steal. *For where your treasure is, there also will your heart be.*"

Here is the Kingdom in our midst, teaching us to spurn the lure of earthly treasure, teaching us to love the eternal.

No, this Kingdom of Christ is not a thing of historical record, buried in the intellectual and spiritual debris of 2000 years. It is a thing of flesh and blood, of grace and life.

It is just as much now as it was then: A reason to live and a reason to die.

This Kingdom of Christ is alive in every city and village of the world, where there is a soul given to the love of Christ. It pulsates even where there are no homes ... on the paved highways and the mud roads of the world.

It is an arrow of light into the darkest regions of human existence.

It does not come alive with each dawn ... as though the world of the spirit has a dawn and a dusk. *The life of grace, the love of Christ is timeless.*

The Kingdom, too, is timeless, placeless: wherever the life of baptism and full belief in Christ is lived, professed; wherever there are people marching in the ranks of Christ, stepping to the beat of Christ's drums ... there is the Kingdom.

In the face of antipathy, disbelief, and the narrowness of prejudice, Christ did not speak of all this boldly and clearly from the first.

Gradually he put rock upon rock and when the building was finally completed, it was clear: he had come to establish a new order, a new economy of salvation. He had come to initiate a Kingdom.

In the beginning there was only a vague design, a pencil sketching. The Jews had felt a certain arrogance about their law, and the Scribes and Pharisees guarded every letter of that law with a self-righteous rigidity and a jealousy that earned for them Christ's terrible words: 'whitened sepulchres!' In the thinking and in the dreams of the Jews was a haunting anticipation: the Messiah. How incredulous they would have been if the 'carpenter's son' had told them the stark truth immediately as he had told the woman at Jacob's Well: "I with whom you speak am he."

Their dreams were of a Messiah of sword and flame, marching gallantly at the head of richly arrayed armies, a Messiah of conquest and opulence ...

Certainly not a Messiah who would take poverty by the hand, and tell his people: Here is your queen ... love her and honour her ... Blessed are the poor in spirit ... Blessed are the peacemakers ... Blessed are the clean of heart.

Had Christ, the Messiah of the spirit, met their granite preconceptions head-on, had he revealed himself and unveiled his new economy of grace and redemption too hastily ... Calvary would not have waited; death would have been as inevitable as it would have been immediate.

And so, he did not pour out at once the new mercies for people which he came bearing in his divine hands; a new law of love to replace the old law of exterior conformity, of an eye for an eye and a tooth for a tooth.

To those who perceived, when their minds broke through the veiled imagery and the parables, he had said, (because they knew what he was about), "Blessed are your eyes, for they see; and your ears, for they hear. For amen I say to you, many prophets and just people have longed to see what you see, and they have not seen it; and to hear what you hear, and they have not heard it."

Jesus likened his Kingdom to a person who sowed good seed in his field, and also to a mustard seed and a net cast into the sea. Why?

The Jews were a highly imaginative people with three dimensional minds, not too fond nor too capable of abstract speculation. A field of grain, a mustard seed, a net cast into the sea: there was here something a person can see and touch and smell.

So Christ spoke their language. They perhaps

could not have grasped the paradox of the Kingdom of God having the good and the bad in its embrace, nor the notions of separation, reward, and punishment; far more easily they could understand the notion of "a person who sowed good seed and whose enemies sowed weeds along with the good seed"; far more easily they could see a net being plunged into the sea, bringing up worthy fish, and the unworthy which will be thrown back.

In the parables Christ let the truth seep through to them.

> "The Kingdom of Heaven is likened to a mustard seed ... This is indeed the smallest of all the seeds; but when it grows up it is larger than any herb and becomes a tree, so that the birds of the air come and dwell in its branches." So it would be. He would start with a handful of disciples, a very small beginning, but the Kingdom will be born; and from this smallest of seeds, it shall grow enormously. It shall be: ... a leaven ... a treasure hidden in a field ... a net cast into the sea.

The final masterpiece took form only gradually. Each stroke of the divine artist's brush added a new line of beauty and clarity.

Here was the light of this world appearing to people, revealing to people, according to their capacities, gradually and gently like the diffusing light of the rising sun. Slowly, but surely, the Kingdom was revealed.

Slowly but surely: "Thou art Peter, and upon this rock, I shall build my Church."

Ah! this is it ... his Church.

Calvary would not be enough. Calvary would heal the bleeding wound of Adam. Calvary would open the bolted doors of heaven ...

But to save all people, the merits of his death on the cross would have to be applied, channeled to the souls of people. He must die to save people, and yet: he must live to save men and women.

He must live on, in his Kingdom, in his Church, in order that he might breathe his life into people.

What a mercy, this mercy of God: to channel a participation in his divine life into the hearts and souls of people; to pour lavishly a sharing of the divine into the human receptacle.

Through his Church: great channels of life, of strength, of forgiveness.

The reservoir of Christ's divine wealth so lavishly given to people is not to be measured. People do not plunge their puny yardsticks to sound the depths of infinity.

There shall be, by his coming, abundant life, abundant strength, and abundant forgiveness for all men and women, in all times ... wherever there is an open heart.

But men and women must drink, must seize upon these channels of life, strength, and forgiveness.

There is in the living Kingdom of God a wealth of God's life for the taking, but men and women must make it happen.

We do not gain God's strength and life and forgiveness from the air about us, nor from the imagination within us. The channels at which we drink must be God's channels. And so it is of the greatest importance for men and women to know: where God's channels are!

There can be no human reason for a divine action. We cannot impute human motives to God. His ways are simply not our ways. Still God deals with us, and might I say, works with us as human beings. Mysterious human psychology is no mystery to the maker of human nature. With the words of Christ and the needs of human nature, then, as our guide, we look into the purpose of Christ in founding a kingdom here in this world.

Christ, the eternal stranger at the doors of the world, did not come only to redeem, to give life. *Christ came to teach, to teach people the mind of God.*

He did not take human form only to teach a small class of students in ancient Palestine – the majority of that class would fail in the final test, anyway.

Christ came to teach all people. Christ came to teach you and me.

He poured the wisdom of God into the ears of twelve men.

What I have whispered into your ears, he enjoined, shout from the house tops. "He who hears you hears me!" "Shout what I have told you down the centuries. Be the unfaltering, living voice of 'My Church!' " "The gates of Hell shall not prevail against it."

Under the inspiration of the Holy Spirit, Matthew, Mark, Luke, and John would write down some of his teachings in their gospels.

But ...

A book without a teacher is not enough.

There must be, according to divine wisdom: "The Church of the living God ... the pillar and mainstay of truth!"

A book, we know, can be misinterpreted.

The lines of print can become vague and shadowy, and you and I can wander down the darkened labyrinths of our understanding, and into tragedy.

There must be a living voice to guide us, to hold us in the right way, to take us by the hand when we are tempted to walk from the beaten path into the treacherous jungles of personal, subjective thinking.

There must be a teacher to whom we are responsible.

Oh, certainly there was a textbook, and a good one. The writings of the four, and the letters of Peter, John, and Paul. These wrote what God wanted, and because God wanted, and nothing that God did not want.

Still, there was never anywhere a command from Christ to write.

The command was: to 'preach and teach ...' nowhere to write ... Christ did not call them to be secretaries.

Christ called them to be a 'living voice' ... to be heard till the ends of time. "I will be with you all days, even till the consummation of the world."

A consideration of the role of the Kingdom or Church and the New Testament; the role of the Church and its necessity for salvation.

The life of God is offered to every person.

The living voice of his teaching will be heard till the last echo from the side of the mountain fades into eternal silence on the last day. "Of his Kingdom there shall be no end."

The living teacher will perpetuate in life all his works.

The Church built upon the rock of Peter will use the textbook of the New Testament, but the textbook will belong to the teacher and will be produced by the teaching Church.

It is not contrariwise: The teacher does not belong to the book, nor is the teacher produced by the book.

Christ's Church will be charged with the authority of heaven; with the authority of Christ himself: to teach, to forgive the sins of all, to sanctify the lives of all. And necessarily so.

For Christ wished his Church to be himself, a continuation of himself and his mission. Only this desire of Christ makes any sense out of his question to Saul, who was a vicious attacker of the infant Church: "Why do you persecute me?" "… me?" Christ asked of the man who had never before seen Christ.

Christ wished the temple of his Church to withstand the rumblings of the earth, the battering rains, the gusts and the gales of time.

Christ wanted his Church to be a sturdy shelter for the wayfaring sons and daughters of Adam and Eve.

Oh, this Church would come upon Calvaries of its own, and bleed just as its divine founder and inspiration bled and knew his Calvary.

Yet his Church would be another Christ.

She would speak as 'one having authority' just as this was said of Christ's own speech so truly.

She would be confident that in her words was a divine sureness … a divine support. Christ would himself live in her, guide her destinies, because from the beginning the whole enterprise was his: "As the Father has sent me … so I send you."

———◆◆◆———

"The weak things of this earth God has chosen to confound the strong."

Twelve men ... handpicked by eternal wisdom ... chosen to launch the great ark of salvation ... endowed with powers that would prostrate the angels with awe ... commissioned to reach every nation ... custodians of the Word of God ... protected in their message by the promise of God himself.

Yet, we must not forget, these were men ... capable of misery and cowardice ... capable of high treason to the highest cause of God ... human blood was in their veins, and human fears in their hearts.

These were the chosen instruments of God.

And in their selection, in their commission: A Church.

People may find their way to heaven without embracing that Church, but only if they do not know, only if their eyes are innocently shut and their hearts are good.

But even then: ignorance is not the price or merit of their salvation. Ignorance is a negative thing, a privation of truth. Ignorance is not the food of eternal life. Those who are in such ignorance will live by the food falling from the table of Christ's Church.

They will live by belief in the truths which Christ's Church has kept sacred and intact.

"Whoever will believe will be saved ... who will not believe will be condemned."

The Church of Christ: a fortress in the desert storm. Some are saved in the wake of the winds, not because they were within the fortress of the Church, but because they huddled closely against the protection of her outer walls.

The Church of Christ: an ark in the flood. Some will not drown, not because they were aboard the ark of the Church, but only because they clutched to floating timber which fell from the decks of the ark. "Whoever will believe will be saved ... who will not believe will be condemned."

———◆◈◆———

If Christ really lives today in his Church, and if Christ is really God, then there must be a Church which can alone claim the finger of God in its origins and history. This Church is not twenty centuries away from Christ, but has been living twenty centuries with Christ; or better, he has lived in his Church for twenty centuries. Looking at the life and words of Christ, we would expect these marks to distinguish his Church: Holiness ... growth beyond human explanation ...unity in truth, worship, and obedience ... and a stability in the face of persecution from without and sickness from within. These marks can belong only to the church which God blesses and in which God lives, for these are achievements beyond human capacity. We may find that these marks lead us to a door that we had studiously shunned because we hated the name above that door. But our hatred and prejudice will die quickly if we are convinced that this is where God lives. There follows a consideration of these divine earmarks and the Church.

The finger of God ... an indelible imprint of divine approval, divine life.

Twelve stumbling, stuttering fishermen, taken from their boats and nets to be made 'fishers of men'. They are almost incorrigible in their belief that Christ's empire is to be a worldly empire to rival Rome. They are stupidly persistent in their desire to be 'first' in his Kingdom of material power.

These twelve were given a charter: "All power in heaven and on earth has been given to me. Go therefore and make disciples of all nations, baptising them in the name of the Father, and of the Son, and of the Holy Spirit, teaching them to observe all that I have commanded you; and behold I am with you all days, even unto the consummation of the world."

These twelve fishermen took this charter and took the divine fire into their hands ... hands which reeked of fish ... and they threw the flames forth to all men.

Ten of the twelve gave the scarlet testimony of their blood. They poured that blood into the ground as though it were waste ... and the seeds of a thousand Christians broke through that ground almost at once ... and the more they were eradicated in the Roman arenas, on the burning crosses, by the mouths of the hungry lions, the more gloriously did they multiply.

This divine fire would not be extinguished! "Behold, I am with you all days, even unto the consummation of the world."

Christ present in his Church ... working a thousand miracles in the souls of people ... bringing a countless host of hearts to the dedication of love ... setting afire the souls of people to endure every form of anguish, echoing the cry of St Paul: "It is the love of Christ that drives me on!"

Christ present in his Church ... bringing inspiration to hands and hearts weary with the struggle ... giving birth to a thousand accomplishments, undertaken solely for his love ... making great people with great hearts ... asking much ... receiving more.

Christ present in his Church ... in the Roman dungeons ... in the distant reaches of barbarian lands ... in human hands that wash the wounds of the lepers ... in eyes that flash hope and love and kindness when the tongue has been cut away for whispering his name ...

Christ present in his Church ... in countless thousands of consecrated souls who have lain willingly and joyfully on the fires of sacrifice ... who have made an oblation of their most natural, most ingrained instincts ... who give and do not count the cost ... who labour till all their energy is poured out, asking only for the reward of his love.

Christ present in his Church ... holding steadfastly to the teachings of Christ, when others have protested and departed to try the truth of infinite wisdom in the dimly lit courts of human intelligence ... keeping the sanctity of the home and of marriage inviolable when others have bowed to convention ... Christ present in his Church which is almost alone his champion and defender.

Christ present in his Church ... preserving the goods of justice and charity ... raising high the torch of chastity ... keeping the values of people in line with the values of God.

If Renan was right, "Jesus Christ has become to such a degree the cornerstone of humanity that to take away his name from the world would be to shake it to its foundations ..."

Then we can also say that if we remove Christ's Church then we remove the only certainty in an uncertain world; remove Christ's Church and we take away the only object of trust in a world of mistrust; remove Christ's Church and we take away from an insane world the only guarantee of sanity; remove Christ's Church and the voice of God will be silent forever.

If, indeed, we were to remove the Church, we would go back to the law of the jungle, where size and might are the standards of truth, and where wrong is a lack of animal cunning.

It is reassuring to know that such a day will never be, for: "Behold I am with you all days, even unto the consummation of the world …"

Christ shall live on and always be present in his Church … holding out to us only his cross … meeting our minds undisguised in demands … yet marked by a growth too grand to be mistaken. We water, but God gives the increase. From a handful: a perpetual springtime of bud and blossom and blade of new life. In three hundred years five million new Christians … and in these first three hundred years the price of Christianity was the perpetual risk of one's life … But the Christians' cry was the cry of Christ's triumph:

"We are but of yesterday, and yet we have filled every place among you — cities, islands, fortresses, towns, market places, camps, tribes, town councils, the palace, the senate, the forum. We have left nothing to you but the temples of your gods … Even unarmed and without any uprising, merely as malcontents, simply through hatred and withdrawal, we could have fought against you. For if such a multitude of people as we are had broken loose from you, and had gone into some remote corner of the earth, the loss of so many citizens would certainly have made your power blush for shame ... You would have been exceedingly frightened at your loneliness, at the silence of your surroundings, and the stupor, as it were, of a dead world. You would have had to look around for people to rule; there would have been more enemies than citizens left to you ..." (From Tertullian's Apology).

This was the brag of a Christian, only one hundred and fifty years after the Son of Man had said: "Thou art Peter, and upon this rock I shall build my Church."

This growth was God's growth, God's gift.

Things which are essentially dissimilar cannot be added: a person and a tree are not counted as two something.

And yet, to violate the rule, add these dissimilars together: There is a Church founded by a son of the most despised of races ... the son of a 'carpenter' in a village whose name and location were hidden by the shadows of a nearby mountain; a Church whose first priests and preachers were timid and ignorant Jews, thick-tongued and thick-headed until the Divine Tongues of Fire on Pentecost; a Church to champion chastity, monogamy, meekness, and charity, all rugged doctrines; a Church to be diffused through veins which were stopped up with prejudice, and the anticipation of a Napoleonic Messiah ... through a paganism rigidly frozen:

this was to be a springtime; a Church spreading wildly on the force of love for one man and one ideal; a Church poised and confident under the snarl of Rome's divine despots; a Church opposed at every turn, driven to the wall, gouged and clawed and burned.

Now add these things together. What do you get?

The sum is, according to Euclid: Defeat ... annihilation!

But we check the answer book of history. There the factual answer reads: wild, inextinguishable growth; a unique phenomenon in its propagation without parallel in the story of man. Since Adam, there has not been any story with the grip, the pathos, the drama of this. Psychologically, all was against it. For this to succeed too much of the impossible was necessary.

When you check this against the unbelievable success story of the fortunes of this Church, there is no doubt.

A hopelessly lost cause succeeds with grandiose success. Here is the mark of the divine; here is the finger of God: God's answer to the Christian prayer: "Thy Kingdom come ..." The answer to the prayer of Christ to his Father at the Last Supper: "Yet not for these only do I pray, but for those also who through their word are to believe in me, that all may be one, even as thou, Father, art in me and I in thee; that they also may be one in us, that the world may believe that thou hast sent me … that thou hast loved them even as thou hast loved me."

Christ is present in his Church in still another way: in the oneness and unity of truth; in the oneness of worship; the oneness in the surrender of our dearest liberty – the surrender to conform – in spite of the autonomy which is so natural and so precious to us. There are millions who happily surrender their sovereignty to seek surety in submission, and to merit an eternal reward.

Never could a human enterprise achieve this. Here we look at a unique phenomenon. Here we behold the hand of God. Here we see realised: "I will be with you all days …"

All days … even down through the long years of buffeting storms, storms enough to reface the earth … storms of sickness and revolution within: the sorrowing sons who have abandoned Christ's house, their home … the violent fists of iron constantly throbbing in anger at her door … Indeed, a vanguard, so mighty in mind and matter; politically potent to destroy any natural foe … drawing blood … yet afraid at the sight. This Church, covered with the blood of attack, staggering and almost falling … is, of all things, smiling and confident … looking out to the ends of the world … in apparent defeat, and yet planning new conquests, because: "I will be with you all days …"

The Church of Christ, in all her preaching, in all her teaching, has never claimed to possess all human knowledge, nor does she canonise her total membership. The net cast into the sea will bring in both the good and the bad fish … the good wheat and the weeds will thrive side by side. There will be dead wood; lifeless branches on the tree. Even regarding those who have stood in the place of Peter, James, and John, history will have many sad chapters. The mothering Church will weep for her wayward sons who have gone astray in spite of her maternal love and care.

But for all the tarnish, all the tinsel that should have been gold, the mother is not to be blamed. She will always, just as she always has, say and know that she is divine because a divine hand guides her destinies, just as a divine will gave her life: "I will be with you all days …"

People may leave her sanctuary, and say that she is not a good mother, and even protest to other people that their mother has failed in holiness.

But this is not what they really mean to say.

They really mean that some of her children have not been worthy of their mother. This is a human experience that few have not encountered. We would not think of blaming the mother whose son has disgraced her in spite of her heroic efforts and the sacrifices she has made to help and train that child.

It is a sad thing to see a person walk out of their mother's house and from their Father's love with bitterness in his or her heart. The mother continues to whisper her continual prayers for these sons who have left her in such bitterness, that they may realise what a great loneliness has come into their lives and eagerly seek the road back home.

Christ's Church, like her divine Founder, would also have her Calvaries. Like him she will know what it is to bleed, to be misunderstood, rejected and hated. She will suffer defections from within in her moment of agony. For her, as for Christ, there will be a thousand other Gardens of Olives … a thousand crowns of thorns. She will feel the pain of her Founder's agony, and will herself sweat blood.

But, and this is all important, in one thing she will not be like her Master: She will never die!

She will live on, gloriously surmounting the mighty boulders and the fallen oaks in her path of progress. She will be unafraid, even in her darkest hours, when the sky is opaque and the earth is trembling under her feet. The bright sunshine of confidence is forever in her heart, for over that heart she wears a promise, wears the word of her divine Lord and Master: "Behold I am with you all days, even unto the consummation of the world."

Chapter 5

The Christian Community

It is a byword with the reasonably pious that people have a basic need for religion. The need for religion is, I think, just another way of saying that a person has a innate need for God. But it is more than just this. The mind of a person is made to hold God's truth, and the heart of a person, as Augustine says, does not rest till it rests in God.

At one time or another each of us turns to God with a fervour we did not think was in us. We clutch God in these moments almost as though we had never known him before. But our emotions soon desert us; they wear out and God's vivid presence fades like a star that has shone in the sky for one night only. Our fits of fervour do not yield enough strength for our day to day service of almighty God. We need help. As human, social beings we need a church. We need to kneel down with the people who live around us and to pray as a member of a community. The sense and strength of numbers is in our nature. We need the feeling and support of community worship. We need the example of others. We need heroes we can admire and whom we seek to imitate.

Though we may wait for a long time on the threshold, torn by doubts and indecision, the course of entrance will eventually be clear to us if our minds are open and our hearts are strong with courage.

If we are determined, the grace of God will work in and through us. If we are determined, without a doubt we will find Christ!

We seek shelter.

But we need more than a roof, food, and a garment. Brute beasts have need for these.

We are not mere living things that feel the bite of a winter wind and the pangs of hunger in the pits of our stomachs. There is another hunger in us, a hunger in the deepest pits of our hearts.

The ability to think and desire, as humans think and desire, creates in us a thousand needs of mind and heart; at times a dire loneliness; a need to love and a need to be loved ... a painful need to know what is right and what is wrong, what is really true and good and beautiful.

This is at once the price and the privilege of being human.

The heart is anxious that the mind should find truth. The heart does not rest until the mind finds truth, and then the heart can have its own share of the reward.

This, for most of us, is a sweaty turmoil, and there are a thousand blind alleys ... and human nausea in the human heart at the point of failure.

The need for security is a great need; it is the need for truth.

Truth contents the mind, stimulates the weary heart.

We may not yet have worked out the theory, we may not have settled upon the formula, but our grasping for truth, and the happiness that comes with it, begins with our alarm clock in the morning and ends with the end of our day. We may not even realise.

We count the crimes of society and recount the cruelties and malice of which the human heart has been capable. We throw up our hands and curse self-righteously even though the same seeds of malice lie fermenting within our own fibres.

When these seeds of evil give painful evidence of being alive, and there is no finer thing in our life to keep us inspired, to keep us in love with life, we seek refuge. You and I seek shelter.

We feel drawn to abandon ourselves to a wickedness of one sort or other: to lust, drink, dope, or despair. Or …

We turn to God.

We turn to seek the meaning of life from the maker of life. This moment of communion with God may send tears down the cheeks; it may cause bitter compunction or a warm peace in the heart; or it may even leave the heart a stone, but:

A soundless voice gives us this assurance: it is the right thing.

Let's name it with its right name: in our desperation, we become *spiritual*.

It is not a mask we wear, not a sedative to put our painful desires to sleep. There is no suggestion of hypocrisy. No person has to apologise for leaning on God. In fact, some lean on God because it is fashionable and not because they are helpless creatures.

For us there is a newness about God when we find him.

A new realisation.

It may be that this new finding of God will be a star that shines in the sky for one night only. We shall search and search the sky thereafter to look for a renewal of its comfort and realisation, but the sky is jet ... And the heart is jet.

And it is no wonder.

Ideas of the mind die, unless ... unless we take them out of the mind and put them into our daily lives. We cannot think religiously for long if we do not live religiously.

We cannot say to God: "I have found you ... I shall never unlock my arms" if we do not also find God in daily honesty, daily generosity and daily worship.

We are not made that way.

We are not made to live a contradiction: to

think and feel and love one way, and live another.

Our dear finding of God must be nourished … or it will die.

But we sense this. So we live spiritually. We choke back that cutting word; silence the urges of our flesh; we try to balance the scales of justice and at day's end, we say our good night and our thanks to God.

But in the shock of daily battle the desire becomes thinner and thinner.

Our neighbour does not share our enthusiasm for the scales of justice; the neighbour throttles us with sharp and wounding words. And this, of course, does not help.

We cannot travel alone.

The social instinct in us looks for companionship in this long and difficult journey. Our good night to God does not fan the flame sufficiently to keep it alive.

We need a Church, an organisation and a community.

We know that our enthusiasm for bridge would have died without the bridge club. We know that our interest in tennis or bowling is kept alive by the tennis club, or the Wednesday night competition and social.

And so too our enthusiasm for God will die a gradual death without some organisation, some league, some community, some Church …

It is very simple. We are made that way.

We might easily find ourselves at the church door but may be torn with a thousand doubts about opening that door and going inside. This is a real point of crisis and it can be met successfully only by having a living and a vibrant faith. Jesus praised this faith very highly when he found it but he lamented it when he found it to be lacking.

We may find ourselves asking these questions but then we may be reluctant to empty our hearts; and even those who boast a gargantuan strength and are able to sever their moorings to earth must be compassionate about the reluctance in those of us who are weaker.

We do not have the strength for murder ... to stand up and see the disorderly children we have nourished within our hearts suddenly fall to their deaths.

We might find ourselves standing at the door of Christ's Church with many quarrelsome problems on our mind.

But as we stand at the church door we feel an occasional warm breath escaping and we are cold.

Or we smell the good smell of food and we are hungry. We want that warmth and that food. We want to go inside: to be sheltered ... to be fed.

The hand trembles as it turns the doorknob. Lean, white knuckles shine as the hand grips solidly.

In that moment of hesitation we might take stock and ruminate upon the long journey that has finally brought us to this door.

We might remember the solemn and demanding voice of Christ: "Who do you say that I am?" ... and the eager response of Peter: "Thou art the Christ, the Son of the living God!" ... or the music in the voice of breathless Andrew as he shouted: "We have found the Messiah!"

"Whoever shall believe in me, the same shall be saved!"

We might remember Christ's answer to the question of the Baptist: "The blind see, the lame walk, the lepers are cleansed, the deaf hear, the dead rise, and the poor have the gospel preached to them."

At Capharnaum: "Arise, take up thy pallet and go to thy house.'"

At Naim: "Young man, I say to thee arise!"

At Bethany: "Lazarus, come forth!"

We might consider the tremendous significance of a cross against the sky and an empty tomb.

Over and above these claims, these proofs, we might remember: "Thou art Peter, and upon this rock I shall build my Church!" "The Church of the living God ... the pillar and mainstay of truth!" "He who hears you hears me." "I will be with you all days, even to the consummation of the world."

———◆━◆◆━◆———

All these things might be going through our minds as we stand in the shadow of the Church.

This, we think, is not the work of an impostor. This is not a bubble that will someday suddenly burst.

This door, we think, is God's door. A turning of this doorknob, one all-important step and we will be in God's house.

But in the second between the thinking and the doing: doubt.

What will people say? Parents, children, husband or wife?

Will those we love punish our convictions and courage with a 'human exile'?

This step we contemplate is permanent ... Faith which proceeds only on a money-back guarantee is unacceptable. God wants more than this of us. Do we have the heart and the hands for this sacrifice?

The mind fills up with these doubts.

Faith in the journey and faith that this is the destiny begin now to lose balance, and struggle sets in.

There is a definite sensation of sinking – sinking right here at the very door of survival.

Sinking ... because doubt has been admitted.

The doubt of what will be said, the doubt that our weakness and our habits will cripple our good will and good intentions ... the terrifying doubt that if we enter beyond that door: we will be lonely.

The strong legs, those which carried us here, are now weak.

The heart is a rattling thing inside. We are abandoned and we are sinking.

———◆·❀·◆———

Conclusion: The answer to doubt and indecision as learned from the time when Christ walked upon the waters of Genesareth.

St Matthew tells us of the occasion when Jesus fed five thousand people. He had sent the disciples to cross the sea of Galilee before him, so that he could retire into the hills to pray. "But in the fourth watch of the night he came to them, walking upon the sea. And they, seeing him walking upon the sea, were greatly alarmed, and exclaimed, 'It is a ghost!' And they cried out for fear. Then Jesus immediately spoke to them, saying, 'Take courage; it is I, do not be afraid.' But Peter answered him and said, 'Lord, if it is thou, bid me come to thee over the water.' And Jesus said, 'Come!'"

Sometime in the darkness and silence of the

night, this night of our earthly life, when our eyes are held and our minds must work things out with great labour, the invitation is given to each of us.

"Come!" The voice of Christ says it to the human heart.

It is night ... the darkness and the tempest and the uncertainty are all about; there is only one anchor: "Come!"

"Come," Christ says, "come to me, you who labour and are burdened, and I will give you rest."

The hands of Christ, the almighty hands of God, go out to the world! They are the compassionate hands that gave so much comfort to the sick and the suffering in Galilee.

"Come! Come into the sacred shelter of my Church. Come into my house and under my roof. Be among my children. Share the light and the warmth of my hearth's fire, the fire of my heart.

"Come! Come with a large heart, filled with faith in me. Come with a sure trust that it is my voice which brings you here, that it is really to me that you are coming."

"Then Peter got out of the boat, and walked on the water to come to Jesus. But seeing the wind was strong, he was afraid; and as he began to sink he cried out, saying, 'Lord, save me!'"

Lord, save us, save us from the fear that grips

us in this dark night when the wind begins to whip up the churning sea about us and inside us.

Save us from this fear which challenges our faith, for faith alone can keep us from sinking.

Save us from the fears that turn our blood to water, as we think of taking this step out over the water, this step into the house which you have built.

Save us from this human pride, worrying about what people will think or say; from the fear of petty gossip and prejudice; from the fear of becoming an exile; the fear of our own frailty.

Lord, save us from these fears which prevent us from coming to you. Do not let them harass our hearts, or hold back our feet from this step into the warmth and light.

"And Jesus at once stretched forth his hand and took hold of him, saying, 'O you of little faith, why did you doubt?' And when they got into the boat, the wind fell. But they who were in the boat came and worshipped him, saying: 'Truly you are the Son of God.'"

And the man or woman struggling with decision finds that those immortal words of profession in Jesus taste sweet on their lips; they feel the comfort of them in their heart.

I do not know the course of the road I have taken … Perhaps I followed a star that shone in the night sky … Perhaps it was a piper's sweet melody that led me here. It is unimportant.

The important thing is that I am here.

I know whom I have loved. "You are the Christ, the Son of the living God."